NORTH KOREA'S FORCED LABOR ENTERPRISE: A STATE-SPONSORED MARKETPLACE IN HUMAN TRAFFICKING

HEARING

BEFORE THE

TOM LANTOS HUMAN RIGHTS COMMISSION

HOUSE OF REPRESENTATIVES

ONE HUNDRED AND FOURTEENTH CONGRESS

FIRST SESSION

APRIL 29, 2015

ISBN-10   1515302067
ISBN-13   978-1515302063

CONTENTS

WITNESSES

LETTERS, STATEMENTS, ETC., SUBMITTED FOR THE HEARING

APPENDIX

NORTH KOREA'S FORCED LABOR ENTERPRISE: A STATE SPONSORED MARKETPLACE IN HUMAN TRAFFICKING

WEDNESDAY, APRIL 29, 2015

HOUSE OF REPRESENTATIVES
TOM LANTOS HUMAN RIGHTS COMMISSION.
WASHINGTON, D.C.

The commission met, pursuant to call, at 2:30 p.m., in Room 2123 Rayburn House Office Building, Hon. Joseph R. Pitts [co-chairman of the commission] presiding.

MR. PITTS. Ladies and gentlemen, I now call this hearing to order on "North Korea's Forced Labor Enterprise: A State-Sponsored Marketplace in Human Trafficking."

I apologize for the delay. We have had to back up with the committee hearings and markups today but finally we are here. This hearing will observe the issue of North Korea's overseas worker programs and I would like to start by reading Article I of the United Nations Universal Declaration of Human Rights. Quote, "All human beings are born free and equal in dignity and rights. They are endowed with reason and conscience and should act towards one another in a spirit of brotherhood," end quote.

There are many articles within the Universal Declaration of Human Rights and other human rights instruments that may pertain to the issue we are observing here today. However, I believe Article I of the declaration most profoundly speaks to my concerns, that all human beings are born free. But in the Democratic People's Republic of Korea, individuals are born and subjugated by their government to crimes against humanity. In practice, virtually none of North Korea's residents or citizens can reasonably be assessed as free. The human rights condition in North Korea is grave. Violations by the DPRK are gross, widespread, systematic and continual. To quote from the findings of the United Nations Commission of Inquiry on Human Rights in the Democratic People's Republic of Korea, quote, "The gravity, scale and nature of those violations reveal a state that does not have any parallel in the contemporary world," end quote.

The findings go on to deem the DPRK as seeking to dominate every aspect of its citizens' lives and terrorize them from within. The severity of the human rights situation in North Korea is well known and I applaud the work of the international community including the work of the United Nations for groundbreaking calls for the prosecution of its leaders for crimes against humanity. I also would like to thank the strong support of the U.S. State Department in these efforts.

As the attention to North Korea's human rights situation increases, human rights observers, activists and policy makers have come across a conundrum, that of the issue of North Korea's labor export programs.

Credible reports indicate that the DPRK's "contract workers" are sent to countries in East Asia, Central Asia, Africa and Central Europe and are forced to work while their movements are surveilled by DARK "minders." Workers' salaries are deposited into accounts controlled by the North Korean government, which keeps most of the money, claiming various "voluntary" contributions to government endeavors. Workers receive only a fraction of the money paid to the North Korean government for their work, and while these workers have their rights violated it is thought that some volunteer their service out of desperation to leave the human rights condition in which they currently find themselves.

The extent of this problem is difficult to measure. Estimates have placed the amount of workers entered into these bilateral contracts anywhere from 20,000 to 100,000 people across the globe. Notably, some observers have objected to the characterization of these workers as forced laborers or victims of human trafficking. It is true that in a cruel irony many of these laborers may be living in better conditions than if they were still residing within the People's Republic of North Korea. However, in response, I fall back upon my earlier citing of Article I of the United Nations Universal Declaration of Human Rights that all human beings are born free and equal in dignity and rights.

The assessment that these laborers are simply acting out of their own self-interest is shortsighted. Although this work abroad may be attractive to the average North Korean, it is only due to the gross human rights violations being perpetrated by the regime in Pyongyang. I would add emphasis to the kind of violations that make such acts of forced labor relatively more attractive -- restrictions of access to food, resulting in mass starvation, the establishment of prison camps, torture, inhumane treatment, arbitrary detention, violations of freedom of religion and expression and other violations that constitute crimes against humanity.

Through the testimony of our witnesses and questions by our commissioners, this hearing hopes to explore the causes and consequences of North Korea's use of forced labor abroad. Its utilization of a revenue generator to an oppressive totalitarian regime as well as what the United States can do to protect these victims of state-sponsored slave labor.

I would like to thank all of our witnesses including Ambassador King for their participation today and look forward to their testimony and recommendations. Our distinguished go-chair, Jim McGovern, will not be able to make the hearing now but we will have his opening statement added to the record.

We have two panels before the commission today and at this time I will introduce the first panel, which is Mr. Robert King, special envoy for North Korea human rights issues, U.S. Department of State. He has served in that capacity since November of 2009. Prior to his appointment, Ambassador King was chief of staff to Congressman Tom Lantos for 24 years. So you are familiar with the situation we find ourself in today, I am sure. It is only fitting that he would find himself here today. He holds a Ph.D. from the Fletcher School of Law and Diplomacy.

Ambassador King, thank you very much for your patience, for appearing before us today and at this point the chair recognizes you for your opening statement.

Prepared Statement of Rep. James P. McGovern

Good afternoon.

I join my colleague and Co-Chair, Congressman Joe Pitts, in welcoming all of you to the Tom Lantos Human Rights Commission's hearing on "North Korea's State-Sponsored Forced Labor Enterprise: Exposing the World's Human Trafficking Marketplace." I thank all of our witnesses for their presence today, and I also want to thank the staff of the Commission, especially Carson Middleton, for organizing this important hearing.

North Korea has a deplorable, perhaps unparalleled human rights record. It is a totalitarian state that tortures and imprisons tens of thousands of people, and prohibits freedom of thought and expression. The regime's apparent single-minded focus on preserving its own power comes at the cost of failing to provide for some of the most basic needs of its citizens, including food and nutrition. In part through its stringent control of engagement with the outside world, and in part because the global community has not made human rights in North Korea a priority, the country has been able to continue this horrific pattern of abuses for decades without facing any significant consequences.

Last year, for the first time, the United Nations conducted an official inquiry into North Korea's human rights situation. In February 2014, the UN Commission of Inquiry concluded that the regime's actions amounted to crimes against humanity punishable under international law and called for urgent action by the global community. Since then, international pressure has been growing. The UN Security Council, for instance, placed North Korea's human rights record on its agenda for the first time. There is no doubt that significant challenges lie ahead, but a positive step has been taken towards stopping North Korea's widespread and systematic abuses.

Today we would like to build on this momentum by examining North Korea's provision of labor to foreign governments and transnational corporations. Although many of these jobs may initially be attractive to North Koreans eager to boost their families' incomes, more and more reports are emerging that thousands – and perhaps tens of thousands – of North Koreans are sent abroad to work in slave-like conditions. The reports indicate that dozens of countries, including China, Russia, and Qatar are receiving North Korean workers in factories and construction sites. Overseas restaurant jobs appear to be sought after by young North Korean women. But most of the workers' income is confiscated by the North Korean government as a source of much needed foreign currency. Some reports allege that the number of workers has increased rapidly in recent years, as North Korea loses other sources of foreign currency due to tightening international sanctions.

Today I look forward to learning more about the situation of North Korean workers abroad. I am eager to discuss constructive and concrete actions that Congress can take to stop exploitation and trafficking. I also hope to explore this issue as a new point of entry to engage North Korea's overall human rights situation.

Thank you, Mr. Chairman.

STATEMENT OF ROBERT KING, SPECIAL ENVOY FOR NORTH KOREA HUMAN RIGHTS ISSUES, U.S. DEPARTMENT OF STATE

MR.KING. Mr. Chairman, thank you very much for the introduction. I was not only the chief of staff to Tom Lantos but after his death I was the one who actually drafted the House resolution that created the Tom Lantos Human Rights Commission.

It is wonderful to come back and see what has happened to the commission, how well you are carrying on that tradition. It is an honor to be here today.

The Democratic People's Republic of Korea -- North Korea -- has one of the worst human rights record of any country in the world. Not long ago, the Economist Intelligence Unit ranked countries on human rights based on a number of criteria. Of the 167 countries ranked, North Korea was dead last. Freedom House's latest report on freedom in 195 countries categorized North Korea as one of the worst of the worst, one of the ten countries in the world with the lowest rankings in every category on human rights. The Committee to Protect Journalists ranked North Korea and Eritrea as the most censured countries on Earth for freedom of information. The U.S. government's religious freedom report categorizes North Korea as a country of particular concern, a country guilty of particularly severe violations of religious freedom including systematic ongoing egregious violations of religious freedom. We could continue but I think the point is clear. As the commission has requested, I would like to focus particularly on North Korea's record of trafficking in persons including, in particular, forced labor.

The most recent State Department trafficking in persons report presents an excellent summary of the problems of North Korea. The DPRK subjects many of its citizens to forced labor and prison camps and through government contracted labor in foreign countries. The report of the United Nations Commission of Inquiry on Human Rights in the DPRK, which is the most thorough well-researched comprehensive report on North Korea's human rights violations, which was released in March last year, estimates that between 80,000 and 120,000 prisoners are held in political prison camps in remote areas of the country. In many cases, these prisoners have not been formally charged with a crime or prosecuted, convicted or sentenced under any legal proceeding. The Commission of Inquiry included that prisoners are subject to deliberate starvation, forced labor, executions, torture, rape as well as forced abortion and infanticide.

A few of the individuals who have survived these prison camps and escaped from the North have written memoirs detailing the horrors of what they have endured. Well-researched reports have been published, which include satellite images that confirm these prisoner accounts. David Hawk's "Hidden Gulag," which was published by the Committee for Human Rights in North Korea, links these personal accounts of prisoners with the satellite images to give a solid and sordid picture of these evil camps. The camps are located in areas where extractive industries or agriculture is carried out. Prisoners are forced to work long hours. They are provided with little food. Living conditions are horrendous. They are not compensated and they under constant surveillance and abuse by brutal guards. In addition to these forced labor camps, the North Korean government also sends large numbers of laborers to work abroad under bilateral contracts with foreign governments and with companies -- foreign companies. It includes a significant number of laborers sent to Russia where large numbers work in logging and construction and agriculture. Many go to China where they work in textile manufacturing and restaurant businesses. The DPRK also has been identified with contracts for workers in Africa, Central Europe, the Middle East, Central Asia and Mongolia.

North Koreans sent to work abroad under these contracts are subjected to forced labor. Their movement communications are conducted under strict surveillance by North Korean government minders. North Koreans sent overseas do not have a choice in the work that the government assigns them and they are not free to change jobs. These workers face threats of government reprisals against them or against their relatives who remain in North Korea if they attempt to escape or complain to outside individuals. Wages of some of the North Koreans workers abroad reportedly are withheld until the laborers return home. Furthermore, the North Korean government skims off a substantial portion of their earnings for its own purposes.

There are other aspects of trafficking including sexual trafficking. I think the focus of your hearing today is not on these issues and I think probably the best thing for me to do at this point is give you an opportunity to ask questions about the concerns that you have raised in your opening statement and that I have raised in my statement as well. There may be issues of particular concern that we can dwell on that will provide, hopefully, some more information about where we should go.

**********COMMITTEE INSERT**********

MR. PITTS. The chair thanks the gentleman.

I do have some questions for you, Mr. Ambassador. First, to what extent has the State Department's annual TIP report -- the Trafficking in Persons report -- and subsequent sanctions process had an effect on North Korea behavior and response to combating human trafficking? To what extent are the United States anti-trafficking efforts limited by the limited presence of foreigners in North Korea? Can you evaluate that for me?

MR.KING. First of all, with regard to the State Department reports, I used to be here on the Hill, as you know. We were always very careful about looking at the State Department reports, the annual report on human rights conditions. While I was here, Congress adopted legislation establishing the Trafficking in Persons report and the religious freedom report. All three of those reports are, I think, an extremely important exercise in terms of identifying where the problems are in terms of human rights conditions. The advantages of these reports are done every year. They are done on a consistent basis and they have reached a high level of credibility in terms of the information that they provide. So I think that the importance of these reports in naming and shaming the violators of human rights is extremely important.

The second question you raise is the question about whether the presence of foreigners in North Korea might improve the situation in terms of information that we have about North Korea. There are very few foreigners that reside in North Korea. The numbers are very limited. The North Koreans make it difficult to stay there. It is particularly difficult for American citizens. There are very few Americans who live in North Korea and who are there longer than a few weeks or a month at a time. It is helpful to have those people there because they do provide information. There are accounts that appear of life in North Korea, what conditions are like there. We find that very helpful and it is very useful.

In terms of labor conditions, I think that is one where it is more difficult. The North Koreans tend to be very careful in terms of controlling what foreigners see when they are in North Korea. When you are there, North Koreans provide you with official minders who are with you the entire time that you are there. I was in North Korea once with Congressman Lantos and I was there when we were having discussions with the North Koreans three or four years ago. We weren't on our own. We couldn't wander the streets freely and have conversations. It was, very clearly, a very controlled situation. Most people who visit North Korea do not get outside of Pyongyang, which limits their ability to know what is going on outside the capital. So having foreigners there doesn't make a big difference in terms of a lot of information that we get but it does help because it provides more information that we would have otherwise. On the other hand, the United States also been very concerned about Americans in North Korea because a number of them have been detained for various reasons and the State Department travel warning on North Korea states explicitly we do not -- we do not encourage Americans to travel to North Korea, period.

MR.PITTS. All right. Thank you.
Has the U.S. government taken any actions or delivered any demarches to governments that have relations with the U.S. but also host North Korean overseas laborers? For example, there are reports that a number of North Korean laborers are working on construction projects in Kuwait and on mines in Malaysia. Has the U.S. government delivered demarches accordingly?

MR.KING. One of our difficulties is finding out what is going on in these places. It is hard for us to have the information. Before we are able to provide -- to issue a demarche or request additional information we need to have a little bit to work on. We are working on that. Where we hear reports we try to find out what has been going on. Unfortunately, many of the areas where these workers go are areas which are not terribly transparent. Russia and China are two of the largest employers of foreign labor and it is very difficult to find information about what is going on in those countries in areas like this.

MR.PITTS. Even in countries like Kuwait or Malaysia?

MR.KING. Kuwait -- we have a good relationship with Kuwait and we are in the process of looking at what the -- what the possibilities are there, what is going on there. Again, in some of these cases the agreements are not with the government directly but with private companies and it makes it more difficult for us to get the information. But yes, we are looking at these issues.

MR.PITTS. All right.
How much evidence is there that North Korea's labor export programs violate United Nations Security Council resolutions such as those banning the transfer of bulk cash to North Korea?

MR. KING. We are not sure, again, because of the lack of information. Foreign labor -- North Korean labor working outside the country does not appear to be a violation of the sanctions. There is a question in terms of how they are paid and how that -- those funds get back. There was a report that recently appeared which suggested that one of the countries involved was paying the North Koreans in product rather than in cash so that they were shipping in food products to North Korea rather than shipping in cash. In terms of transfers of funds into North Korea, we watch that very carefully and very closely. The Treasury Department is looking very carefully at what is done in terms of attempts to violate sanctions with bank transfers and so forth. We have managed in a number of cases to identify problems and I think we have made some -- we have had some success in terms of dealing with those issues.

MR. PITTS. Aside from the TIP report, what tools does the U.S. government have to pressure host countries to improve conditions for overseas North Korean workers and/or end these programs altogether?
Are there examples of governments taking these types of actions in response to U.S. pressures?

MR. KING. Most of the countries that have problems or where there are reports that there are North Korean laborers are not countries that are transparent and open in terms of their economy and it makes it difficult for us in terms of identifying what might be done. The one thing that I think we do that is helpful is through the use of reports, through the use of information that we disseminate, is to name and shame violators who are guilty of these kinds of human rights abuses. For better or for worse, there is an effect when we call attention to these violations. One of the things we have spent a considerable amount of time and effort dealing with is getting other nations to join us in the United Nations and the Human Rights Council and the General Assembly, and last year in the Security Council, to raising the issues of North Korea's human rights violations. Included in that are the forced labor issues that we have been talking about, and by raising these issues and the United Nations has adopted a number of resolutions that deal with this issue, among others, I think we have had some success at affecting the North Koreans. It is very clear over the last year the appearance of the report from the Commission of Inquiry has led the North Koreans to be much more sensitive about the human rights issue. The resolution that was adopted by the General Assembly, the resolution that was adopted by the Human Rights Council called for a referral of the North Korean issue to the International Criminal Court. This got the attention of the

North Koreans. They have been much more aggressive in terms of fighting back but also in terms of trying to get their case out there. They are feeling the pressure and it is our intention, certainly, to continue to press them.

MR. PITTS. Has the North Korean government sent more workers abroad since Kim Jung-un took power in late 2011? Are there indications that these workers are bringing in more or less revenue than earlier years? Can you estimate the annual revenue from overseas labor programs?

MR.KING. There are some off the top of the head suggestions that have very little basis in fact. Very difficult to get these kinds of numbers. In terms of looking at what has happened over time, we think that there is less use of North Korean labor in places like Eastern Europe than there was ten years ago or 15 years ago. So we believe there has been an effect in terms of publicizing what has been going on. In terms of identifying whether the numbers have increased or not, hard to tell. My best guess, based on what I have seen, is that in Russia there probably has been some increase in the number of North Korean laborers that are working in agriculture and forestry and construction. There has probably been an increase in terms of numbers working in China of textile industry, construction possibly, certainly in terms of the restaurant business. So there is probably a few more in those areas. But in terms of giving you an order of magnitude, we don't have the data that will confirm that.

MR.PITTS. Some would allege that there are signs that North Korea is opening up its economy and point to North Korea's expansion of operations in neighboring countries as evidence of entrepreneurial endeavors.
Do you assess that North Korea is opening up its economy?

MR. KING. There certainly have been economic changes that have taken place in North Korea. Up until the mid-1990s, basically North Koreans were provided food -- the government provided food. When you went to work you were given a chit that you could take to the public distribution center and receive a certain amount of rice and other things. With the famine of the 1990s, the collapse of the public distribution system, it is now estimated that most of the food that is consumed in North Korea is purchased in markets. There are limited markets. They are regulated by the government. But the most recent number that I have seen is that 80 percent of the food that is purchased by North Koreans is bought in open markets. So the economy is becoming somewhat more market oriented. The market also appears to have more connections with China and there are consumer goods and other products that are coming in from China so that the market changes are probably positive. In terms of major changes, there is still a long way to go.

MR. PITTS. Credible reports have indicated that middlemen are helping cover the tracks of North Korea's overseas labor efforts, making it impossible to tell that products are made with North Korean hands to contribute to North Korean profits.
Can you tell us about any evidence of efforts by firms to hide North Korean involvement?

MR. KING. This is something that we would pay fairly careful attention to. Usually, however, and you are getting into an area that is probably a little beyond my expertise. This is a trade issue. We tend to be careful about the country of origin. We tend to be less careful about the nationality of laborers who work on products that might be exported. So I think that is something that would be very hard to identify and very hard to deal with.

MR. PITTS. In your opinion, is the growth of North Korean overseas labor operations an indication of the success of international sanctions?

MR. KING. I think it is unrelated to international sanctions. I think the international sanctions on North Korea have limited very seriously efforts by the North Koreans to bring in certain goods that are covered by sanctions. The sanctions primarily are focused on nuclear weapons, materials that would be necessary for nuclear and other weapons systems and I think we are paying very careful attention to what goes on in that regard.
The sanctions don't cover food and other kinds of goods that are, you know, for the well being of the population. The difficulty for the North Koreans is they don't have money.
The North Korean economy is not a robust economy. When you look at South Korea, South Korea is one of the wealthiest countries and one of the most successful economically in the world as a member of G-20. It has a high standard of living. When you look at North Korea, which has a population of only half the size of South Korea, North Korea's economy is one-fortieth the size of South Korea.

So we are talking about a country that is on the level of a sub-Saharan African country in terms of the size of its economy. This is not a wealthy country, although there are a few people there who do live very well.

MR. PITTS. Okay. Finally, how would you characterize the overseas worker programs? Do they constitute human trafficking? Is this slave labor? Would you consider this to be a form of state-sponsored human trafficking? Would you characterize it, please?

MR. KING. We are getting into definitional issues. I would call it bad and I would call it something that we need to be concerned about because these are people who are being exploited. These are people who are being sent overseas and they are being controlled because they have family members who remain in Korea. They have control over what they do and where they go and what kinds of things they are able to do in these countries. They are also given only a portion of the wage they earn because there is a certain amount that is skimmed off by the North Korean government under terms of their contracts. So yes, this is certainly exploitation of these workers. It is the kind of thing that is certainly a violation of the Universal Declaration of Human Rights. It is a violation of the rights that most countries of the world have subscribed to in the Convention for the International Labor Organization. So yes, it is a problem. It is a violation of international obligations. Does it meet the definition of trafficking? Does it meet the definition of forced labor? In my mind, it is probably pretty close.

MR. PITTS. Thank you, Mr. Ambassador. We will have follow-up questions for you. I am sure members who have been detained in other meetings will have written questions. I will send them to you in writing. If you would please respond we would appreciate it.

MR. KING. Be happy to respond. Thank you very much.

MR. PITTS. Thank you very much, Mr. Ambassador. Thank you for your patience. So we will dismiss Panel I and I will now call Panel II to the witness stand and staff, you can make sure they have their appropriate designations.

On Panel II, I will introduce them in order of them speaking. First, Mr. Greg Scarlatoiu, executive director, Committee for Human Rights in North Korea; secondly, Mr. Lim Il, co-director, International Network for the Human Rights of North Korean Overseas Labor; and then Mr. John Sifton, Asia advocacy director of Human Rights Watch.

And I will now introduce each of them on our second panel. These are distinguished witnesses.

Mr. Greg Scarlatoiu serves as the -- as I said, executive director of Committee on Human Rights in North Korea. He holds a Master of Law and Diplomacy from the Fletcher School as well as an MA from Seoul National University. Mr. Scarlatoiu is a distinguished lecturer on North Korea and human rights and is currently working on a report on the topic that we are covering today, which will be published late this summer.

We have Mr. Lim Il, co-director of the International Network for Human Rights of North Korean Overseas Labor. Mr. Il formerly held a prestigious job with a North Korean construction company. He decided to defect in 1997. A published author, Mr. Il heads the network and is dedicated to exposing North Korea's exploitation of its own citizens via the slave labor system.

And finally, Mr. John Sifton is the Asia advocacy director of Human Rights Watch. He holds his law degree from the New York University. He has testified before this commission numerous times in the past.

So Mr. Sifton, thank you for appearing before us today, and I would like to thank all of the witnesses for your participation in the hearing today. So we will begin. Do you have a different order? Was the order I gave you okay?

Mr. Greg Scarlatoiu, you are recognized for your opening statement, and make sure you push the button. Yes. Thank you.

STATEMENTS OF GREG SCARLATOIU, EXECUTIVE DIRECTOR, COMMITTEE FOR HUMAN RIGHTS IN NORTH KOREA; LIM IL, CO-DIRECTOR, INTERNATIONAL NETWORK FOR HUMAN RIGHTS OF NORTH KOREAN OVERSEAS LABOR; JOHN SIFTON, ASIA ADVOCACY DIRECTOR, HUMAN RIGHTS WATCH

STATEMENT OF MR. SCARLATOIU

MR. SCARLATOIU. Good afternoon, Chairman Pitts. On behalf of the Committee for Human Rights in North Korea, I would like to express my great appreciation for inviting me to speak with you today about North Korea's forced labor enterprise and its state sponsorship of human trafficking.

North Korea's exportation of forced laborers to foreign countries earns the Kim regime the hard currency critical to its survival. Recent estimates indicate that there are currently over 50,000 North Korean laborers working overseas, earning the Kim regime between $1.2 billion and $2.3 billion a year. The program began with the exportation of labor to the Soviet Union, to the far east of the Soviet Union in 1967. North Korean workers have been sent to 45 countries in Asia, Africa, the Middle East and Europe. Currently, 16 countries are hosting North Korean workers. Although North Korea is not a member of the International Labor Organization, all but two of the 16 states are ILO members.

The regime selects male candidates of good songbun, North Korea's loyalty-based social discrimination system, married with at least one child. They are on the fringes of the so-called core class -- loyal but poor. Young women sent overseas as restaurant workers come from privileged core class families. Previously, the ambitions of those dispatched overseas were modest. In the last 1980s, a North Korean I met worked as a logger in the Russian far east to give his family a color TV. Ultimately, he never saw them again.

To go overseas, workers have to give a $100 to $200 bribe, liquor, cigarettes or dining coupons at high-end restaurants to those making the selection. After they cross the border, their passports are confiscated by their minders. In the 1980s and early 1990s, the workers' families received not money but coupons to purchase food and electronics. In the 1990s, the coupon system collapsed and the number of overseas North Korean workers declined. As the number began increasing again, the workers gained limited access to opportunities to earn cash. With the approval of the three site supervisors, the Workers Party secretary, the State Security Department -- SSD agent -- and the work site manager, they may moonlight or be subcontracted by other foreign workers if they bribe their bosses.

The North Korean worker ends up being exploited by his government, by the recipient country, by his supervisors and by other foreign workers. The loyal pauper is at the bottom of the heap and the Kim regime knows it. Upon his return to North Korea, the State Security Department keeps him under strict surveillance for at least three years. The workers abroad do not have any freedom of association or collective bargaining.

Which then results in swift repatriation and harsh punishment. The selection of young women only for restaurant jobs overseas amounts to severe gender discrimination. Social discrimination is rampant. Only those of good songbun are sent overseas.

Health and safety violations are widespread. The scale of health and safety violations and the frequency of workplace accident-related injuries and fatalities may vary depending on location, industry and specialization. The fatality rate is high among loggers.

Wage violations are rampant. Workers are not paid directly by their foreign employers. The workers don't even know what overtime work means. The laborers work between 14 and 16 hours a day with no holidays except perhaps one day a month. In most cases, the working conditions amount to forced labor. It is only the scale that may differ, depending on the recipient country, industry and specialization. Differences in the scale of forced labor are circumstantial rather than intentional.

To improve the working conditions and human rights of North Korean workers residing overseas the following recommendations are offered.

First, North Korea should abide by its obligations under the International Covenant on Civil and Political Rights to which it acceded in 1981 and its own domestic legislation to protect the rights of its workers at home and abroad. Second, the eight ILO core conventions should be the minimum standard applied to determine the status of overseas North Korean workers and to hold both North Korea and receiving countries accountable. Third, a set of standards inspired by the global Sullivan principles should be developed. Companies along the supply chain tainted by violations of the rights of exported North Korean workers should abide by those standards. Fourth, further investigation of the situation of exporting North Korean laborers should be conducted and the cooperation of host countries should be sought. Fifth, a determination should be made in the presence of tens of thousands of North Korean citizens overseas may provide opportunities for access and interaction despite draconian control and surveillance. Sixth, awareness campaigns to stimulate grass roots advocacy. Seventh, North Korea should join the ILO and apply internationally accepted minimum core labor standards to protect its workers at home and abroad. Eighth, countries where North Korean laborers reside should take steps to protect the rights of all foreign workers including North Korean workers. Ninth, hosting states should conduct schedules and surprise inspections of work sites employing North Koreans pursuant to their international obligations. Tenth, hosting states and employers should seek direct access to North Korean workers and distribute material informing them on their rights. Eleventh, violations of the labor rights of North Korean workers residing overseas should be included in future legislation pertaining to sanction regimes. Twelfth, the exportation of North Korean labor should be terminated through concerted international action if the North Korean regime refuses to improve the working conditions and the overall human rights situation of its workers.

Thank you, Chairman Pitts. I look forward to answering any questions you might have.

[The statement of Mr. Scarlatoiu follows:]

Good afternoon, Chairman Pitts. On behalf of the Committee for Human Rights in North Korea, I would like to express great appreciation for inviting me to speak with you today about North Korea's forced labor enterprise and its state sponsorship of human trafficking. It is an honor and a privilege to have an opportunity to discuss these issues with you today.

North Korea's "Royal Palace Economy"

North Korea's nuclear and missile developments and other military provocations have continued to threaten international peace and security and challenge U.S. foreign and security policy. The Kim regime's ruthless prevention and suppression of dissent among its population, isolation from the outside world, and denial of fundamental human rights have all worked to undermine peace and security on the Korean peninsula. Meanwhile, the "royal palace economy" (a term coined by HRNK non-resident fellow Kim Kwang-jin) generating hard currency for North Korea's leaders has continued to enable three generations of Kims to stay in power through, in part, exploitation of its people sent to work overseas. North Korea's exportation of tens of thousands of workers to foreign countries is an important part of the hard currency generating apparatus employed to sustain the Kim regime and (relatively) one of its more transparent examples of clear human rights violations against its people. Understanding this and the other building blocks of the "royal palace economy" will enable a better discernment of the reasons behind the longevity of the regime. It will also allow for the preparation of more effective sanctions to address the security and human rights challenges the regime poses, thereby improving the human rights situation of North Koreans.

The essential goal of the North Korean Human Rights Act of 2004 and the Reauthorization Acts of 2008 and 2012 is to promote respect for the fundamental human rights of the North Korean people. Enhanced understanding of North Korea's quasi-licit and illicit international economic activities and their connection to human rights will enable experts, policymakers, and the public to more effectively seek ways to improve the human rights of North Koreans, especially of workers sent overseas.

The international sanctions imposed on North Korea have been based on the threats it has posed to international peace and security, as defined in Chapter VII, Article 41, of the UN Charter. The sanctions have not always been fully effective, primarily due to lack of cooperation by UN member states in the arms area. Effectively documenting linkages between the supply chain of the "royal palace economy" and human rights violations can provide the basis for expanding and diversifying the ground for action beyond existing North Korea sanctions.

In December 2014, following a February 2014 landmark report by a UN Commission of Inquiry establishing that the Kim regime has been committing crimes against humanity and subsequent strong UN Human Rights Council and UN General Assembly resolutions on North Korean human rights, this topic was included in the permanent agenda of the UN Security Council. While fully acknowledging the importance of the security challenges North Korea presents, a better understanding of the linkages between the "royal palace economy" and human rights violations, in particular those relating to North Korean workers residing in foreign countries, will continue to help shift international attention and the ground for action to human rights and labor violations committed by the North Korean regime, in particular the exploitation of workers, human trafficking, and forced labor.

The Current Situation in North Korea

In order to maintain itself in power—its main strategic objective, the Kim regime has ruthlessly prevented and suppressed dissent and denied North Koreans their most fundamental human rights. Since the death of Kim Jong-il in December 2011, North Korea has been undergoing its second dynastic transition. After the first three years of Kim Jong-un's rule, the human rights situation has not shown any signs of improvement. Under the new leadership, North Korea also appears to have chosen the same path of brazen provocations and threats to regional peace and security, including missile launches and a nuclear test, undertaken at a cost that could have fed millions of North Koreans for years.

Twenty-six years since the collapse of communism in Eastern Europe, and despite sanctions imposed pursuant to UN Security Council Resolutions, the North Korean regime has managed a second hereditary transfer of power to Kim Jong-un, son of Kim Jong-il and grandson of Kim Il-sung. While the Kim regime has found the resources to produce nuclear weapons, and while it appears that at least some elite residents of Pyongyang enjoy luxury goods imported in violation of UN Security Council sanctions, no fewer than 21 million North Koreans out of a population of 24 million live under dire circumstances.

The 2-3 million North Koreans who are privileged belong to the "core class" according to North Korea's social classification system, *songbun*. Some of them enjoy cell phones, better apartments, and much better living conditions than the 21 million. North Korea's "royal palace economy" is not intended to improve the livelihoods of ordinary North Koreans. Through exports of licit, but especially quasi-licit and illicit goods, the regime seeks to earn currency for itself and for its immediate supporters. This is the purpose also served by North Korean workers exported overseas, who are denied basic labor rights. Because the regime does not show signs of embarking on real reform, the "royal palace economy," including the system of sending workers overseas, can be expected to be relied upon and expanded further.

Overseas North Korean Workers

The North Korean government has earned significant amounts of foreign currency by exporting North Korean laborers. After the collapse of communism in the former Soviet Union and Eastern Europe, the number of North Korean workers dispatched overseas declined. However, in recent years, the number appears to be on the rise, likely as the result of the Kim Jong-un regime's attempts to increase available sources of funding, as it grows more isolated due to its missile and nuclear developments and brazen military provocations combined with the impact of international sanctions.

The North Korean regime recruits workers for assignments overseas under bilateral contracts with foreign governments. North Korean workers arrive in the recipient countries on three to five year contracts that can be extended indefinitely or not at all depending on the performance and loyalty of the worker. Recent estimates indicate that there are currently 52,300-53,100 North Korean laborers working overseas, earning the Kim regime between USD 150 million and USD 230 million per year.[1] Available

---

[1] International Network for the Human Rights of North Korean Overseas Labor (INHL). *The Conditions of the North Korean Overseas Labor*. INHL. Seoul. 2012 (hereinafter "INHL Report"). Note: Estimates of the number of North Korean workers overseas vary. For example, UN Special Rapporteur Marzuki Darusman reported the number as approximately 20,000 in a news conference on March 16, 2015. *See* Stephanie Nebehay, *U.N. Expert to Probe Conditions of North Korean Workers Abroad*, 16 March 2015, REUTERS, http://www.reuters.com/article/2015/03/16/us-northkorea-workers-

reports indicate that the first overseas North Korean laborers were loggers exported to the Soviet Far East in 1967.[2] Since the inception of the program, North Korean workers have been officially dispatched to 45 countries in Asia, Africa, the Middle East and Europe.[3] Currently, 16 countries reportedly host workers sent by the North Korean regime: Russia (20,000), China (19,000), Mongolia (1,300), Kuwait 5,000), UAE (2,000), Qatar (1,800), Angola (1,000), Poland (400-500), Malaysia (300), Oman (300), Libya (300), Myanmar (200), Nigeria (200), Algeria (200), Equatorial Guinea (200) and Ethiopia (100).[4] Although North Korea is not a member of the International Labor Organization (ILO), all 16 states officially hosting North Korean workers are ILO members.

Initially, North Korean loggers were sent to the former Soviet Union as part of a crude barter: North Korean labor, often forced, in exchange for Soviet weapons and some goods for civilian use, such as rudimentary electronics. In the 1970s and especially in the 1980s, as the economic situation of North Korea was becoming dire, the workers "realized that Russia was a better place as soon as they crossed the border."[5] The regime realized that, however difficult the working conditions may have been even in the Russian Far East, the situation at home was worse, and the workers may have been tempted to defect. Thus, the regime decided to select male candidates of good *songbun,* married with at least one child, but more often with two or more. One's belonging to the "core" class of certified loyalists and the family left behind was meant to deter defection. Certainly, none of them belonged to the *crème de la crème* of highly privileged Kim regime loyalists. They were on the fringes of the "core" class, loyal and employed in "respectable" positions, but poor. This remains the case today and also applies to young women now sent overseas as restaurant workers. Most of them have come from privileged "core" class families. Young women of good *songbun* have also been recently dispatched to work in China's textile industry.

Their Motives

Previously, the ambitions of those workers dispatched overseas were modest. For example, HRNK interviewed a former North Korean worker who, in the late 1980s, chose to work as a logger in the Russian Far East for two years. He agreed to work in substandard conditions, hoping that upon his return he would be able to "improve his family's life, by offering them a color TV." His fellow loggers were there for similar reasons, he said. However, in his and other cases, they never saw their families again as a result of the great famine and death toll in North Korea. This worker—and doubtless others—defected from the

---

idUSKBN0MC24420150316. People for Successful Corean Reunification (PSCORE) estimated the number between 50,000 to 150,000 in a written statement submitted to the UN Human Rights Council. *See* A/HRC/28/NGO/51, 20 February 2015, http://ap.ohchr.org/documents/dpage_e.aspx?c=50&su=59.

[2] *Logjams in the Soviet Timber Industry.* A research Paper. U.S. Central Intelligence Agency. Directorate of Intelligence. SOV 83-10206X. December 1983. Declassified in part, sanitized copy approved for release, January 26, 2012.

[3] Shin, Chang-Hoon and Myong-Hyun Go. *Beyond the UN COI Report on Human Rights in DPRK.* PP 21. The Asan Policy Institute. 2014.

[4] Ibid.

[5] HRNK interview with former North Korean logger in Russia. July 2013.

logging camp when he could no longer manage to help his family. He wandered around Russia for years, before finally finding his way to South Korea.[6]

Currently, North Korean workers may volunteer to go overseas in hope of better opportunities; they may be sent by their state companies on their accord; or they may just be dispatched by their employers, regardless of their preferences.[7] Nowadays, as reliance on markets has increasingly replaced the Public Distribution System (PDS), money plays a more prominent role in North Korea, and more workers seek overseas positions hoping for better opportunities than those available at home.

The agencies in charge of sending workers overseas may differ. Some of the construction workers exported to the Middle East are sent through Pyongyang Overseas Construction Enterprise. Loggers are sent to the Russian Far East by the Forestry Department. Since "North Korea has to select the ones [workers] of good *songbun,* the Social Safety Agency takes charge of the background investigation."[8]

If a worker wants to go overseas, he has to bribe those involved in the selection process. Some workers mentioned USD 100-200, a very hefty amount by North Korean standards. One of them said it cost him a carton of cigarettes and two high quality liquor bottles. In order to secure an overseas deployment of up to three years, the selection process can be rather complicated:

"The difficult thing was that we had to have seven people as guarantors, so I asked my wife, older brother, the president of my company, manager, the party secretary, the State Security Department agent in charge of managing my company, and a police officer (Ministry of Public Security agent) to do it for me. After I reported seven guarantors on the application document, they gave me the authorization stamp which allowed me to leave."[9]

Prior to their departure, the workers undergo indoctrination sessions and a physical examination. The physical examination, generally done no sooner than six months prior to departure, involves a blood test and eye, ear, and liver examination. The regime wants no medical expenses during their stay overseas, so only workers in excellent health are sent. As soon as they cross the border, their minders confiscate their passports. They will see them again only right before boarding the plane taking them back to North Korea, or right before crossing the land border from China or Russia.

In the 1980s and early 1990s, the overseas workers did not receive money for their work. Instead, their families received coupons which they could in turn use to purchase food and coveted washing machines or color TV sets from special stores. As the great famine of the mid to late 1990s set in, this system collapsed, together with the PDS. However, loggers and other workers still had to work for no pay. Through the few letters received from home, they learned that families continued to receive the coupons, but they were useless, as stores were now empty. As their families starved, some of these hardened men, who had survived appalling working conditions, decided to assume the ultimate risk: they left the logging

[6] HRNK interview with former North Korean logger in Russia. July 2013.

[7] *Pukhan Haewoe Nodongja Inkwon Shilthae* (The Current Human Rights Situation of North Korean Workers Dispatched Overseas). PP 41. Database Center for North Korean Human Rights. Seoul. 2015.

[8] HRNK interview with former North Korean construction worker in the Middle East.

[9] HRNK interview with former North Korean logger in Russia. July 2013.

camps, desperate to find a way to help their dying families. Even most of those who ultimately found their way to South Korea or other third countries were never reunited with their families again.

Two of the former restaurant workers interviewed, graduates of both college and Sojo (performing arts "institute"), stated that they wanted to work overseas "to see the world, and didn't think much about the pay."[10] Secluded in their living quarters and workplace almost the entire time, they only seldom got away for a few hours, to shop at local markets, under the constant surveillance of colleagues and minders.

During and after the great famine, the number of overseas North Korean workers declined. As the number began increasing again during the final years of the Kim Jong-il regime, at some locations, in particular in the Russian Far East (Khabarovsk and Vladivostok) and the Middle East, North Korean workers gained very limited access to opportunities to make a little money for themselves. In order to do that, one has to be cleared by the three supervisors: the Workers' Party secretary—90 percent of the workers are party members, the State Security Department (SSD) agent, and the worksite manager.

The reason why some of the workers – even the most trusted – are cleared is that supervisors are increasingly corrupt and interested in extracting some profits for themselves. When a worker is sent abroad, he may be allowed by his supervisors to be "subcontracted" by other foreign workers at the same site. In such cases, other North Korean workers at the site have to increase their already overwhelming level of effort to make up for his absence. South Asian construction workers in the Middle East are known to "subcontract" North Korean workers to do their job. A foreign worker getting paid USD 40 a day hires the North Korean to do his job, paying him only half the daily wage. The respective foreign worker is free to work another job, thus increasing his income. The North Korean is left with very little, as he has to share the USD 20 with the three supervisors. The North Korean worker ends up being exploited by his government, by the recipient country—which is ultimately responsible for enforcing the labor rights of foreign workers within its territorial jurisdiction, by his three worksite supervisors, and even by other foreign workers. The loyalist pauper is now at the bottom of the heap, and the Kim regime knows it. Upon their return to North Korea, the SSD keeps the workers under strict surveillance for at least three years.

Working Conditions

As a state party to the International Covenant on Civil and Political Rights (ICCPR), North Korea legally takes upon the responsibility to not undertake forced labor or servitude.[11] The international community expects North Korea to observe ICCPR Article 8, 3 (a) – that "no one shall be required to perform forced or compulsory labour."[12] North Korea should also observe ICCPR Article 8, 1 prohibiting "slavery" and Article 8, 2 prohibiting "servitude." Newspaper investigations, research reports, testimony from defectors and businessmen, and additional empirical evidence indicate that North Korea violates internationally accepted labor standards in its labor export program. High-profile North Korean defector Kim Tae Sun

---

[10] HRNK interviews with former North Korean restaurant workers. July 2013 and August 2014.
[11] "International Covenant on Civil and Political Rights." Office of the United Nations High Commissioner for Human Rights, http://www2.ohchr.org/english/law/ccpr.htm.
[12] Ibid.

testified before the European Parliament that the coercive nature of North Korea's international labor practices amounted to "21st century slave labor."[13] Even if North Korea's overseas workers did choose to work of their own accord, they are nevertheless made to accept sub-par, coercive working conditions and stay in their jobs through tactics and policies that would be beyond questionable almost anywhere else.

The situation of North Korean workers exported to other countries ranges from cruel and violent acts to ruthless exploitation. At worst, one may end up as a corpse inside a sealed coffin, decaying for months before being repatriated. At best, one may be allowed by the worksite supervisors to moonlight or do a side job in addition to one's own heavy workload in order to earn a very small amount, after having paid the requisite bribes to those in charge.

Former loggers and a former logging camp truck driver told HRNK a terrifying story: When a worker dies at the camp, the body is not automatically repatriated. The cost of fuel is high, so management waits until ten corpses have piled up. Sometimes it takes five months or so. In most cases, the families receive decomposing or already decomposed bodies. The truck driver mentioned the most frightening sound he heard: water sloshing inside the ten sealed coffins he had loaded onto his truck, thawing corpses inside.

Freedom of Association/Collective Bargaining

The European Parliament's 2010 resolution on North Korea asserted that "the government subjects the population to forced labour as part of labour mobilization campaigns, and does not permit free association of labour or collective bargaining."[14] The ILO's Freedom of Association and Protection of the Right to Organise Convention affirms that these rights are fundamental characteristics of a clean supply chain.[15] Available evidence indicates that North Korean workers abroad do not have the freedom to associate with groups and individuals as they choose, or to engage in minimal collective bargaining practices that are prevalent around the world. Additionally, the International Covenant on Economic, Social and Cultural Rights (ICESCR), which North Korea acceded to in 1981, places an obligation on states parties to ensure "the right of everyone to form trade unions and join the trade union of his choice, subject only to the rules of the organization concerned, for the promotion and protection of his economic and social interests."[16]

Preliminary conclusions based on desk research and 25 interviews recently completed by HRNK for an upcoming publication on North Korean overseas workers indicate that they have no right to freedom of association or collective bargaining. Any attempt to protest their working conditions, to strike or organize would result in their swift repatriation and harsh punishment:

---

[13] Demick, Barbara. "N. Koreans Toil Abroad under Grim Conditions." The Los Angeles Times, http://articles.latimes.com/2005/dec/27/world/fg-slaves27.

[14] "European Parliament Resolution on North Korea ". The European Parliament, http://www.europarl.europa.eu/sides/getDoc.do?type=MOTION&reference=B7-2010-0446&language=EN.

[15] "C87 Freedom of Association and Protection of the Right to Organise Convention, 1948". 1948. International Labour Organization. 02/15 2012.
<http://www.ilo.org/ilolex/cgi-lex/convde.pl?C087>.

[16] ICESCR, Article 8, 1 (a),
http://www.ohchr.org/EN/ProfessionalInterest/Pages/CESCR.aspx.

"They put plaster casts on both of the worker's legs and send him back. The casts are taken off after they cross the border. They let the workers go home if it's a minor problem, but for bigger issues they are sent to the *kwan-li-so* (political prison camp)."[17]

In most cases, the working conditions amount to forced labor. It is only the scale that may differ, depending on the recipient country, industry, or specialization. Differences in the scale of forced labor are circumstantial, rather than intentional.

Gender Discrimination

The selection of young women only for restaurant and textile jobs overseas is indicative of deeply embedded gender discrimination for both males and females. Women, for one, tend to be selected to work in overseas restaurants if "you have a pretty face [and] are taller than 1.62 meters [approximately 5'3"],"[18] in addition to having good *songbun* and a Pyongyang education or music degree. For men, overseas labor consists of logging and construction, primarily, requiring extraordinary levels of manual labor over long hours. And despite these factors, the situation inside North Korea is grim enough that North Koreans still believe that temporarily leaving the country may still be an opportunity to have a glimpse of the outside world and send a little money to the family left behind. Further discriminatory practices of only selecting those of good *songbun* amounts to blatant discrimination against those belonging to the "wavering" or "hostile" class based on their perceived lack of loyalty to the regime. Since families are held hostage in North Korea to prevent defection, single men are precluded from access to overseas jobs.

Health and Safety

Health and safety violations are widespread at overseas North Korean worksites. The scale of health and safety violations may depend on location, industry and specialization. Logging camps in Russia may be hours away from emergency care. Such facilities are much closer for those working in urban areas in Russia, China or the Middle East. In the case of female restaurant workers, most of whom are daughters of the elites, the North Korean government will reportedly pay only for appendectomies.[19] If health issues are too serious to be resolved through self-medication, the workers are repatriated.

The frequency of workplace accident-related injuries and fatalities depends on industry and specialization. The fatality rate is high among loggers, in particular among truck drivers—who often have to drive on slippery surfaces—and the teams tasked to cut down the trees. Loggers work at night, with no illumination other than the moonlight, and sometimes truck headlights. Safety training is minimal, and basic safety procedures are often not observed.

Protection of Wages

North Korea most blatantly violates international law and labor standards regarding wages. As mentioned, North Korea acceded to the ICESCR. As such, it has the affirmative duty to adhere to the treaty, which includes Article 7:

---

[17] HRNK interview with former North Korean logger in the Primorsky, Tinda, Amur Oblast, Russian Federation.

[18] INHL Report, *supra* note 1, *at* 33.

[19] HRNK interview with former restaurant worker, August 2014.

The States Parties to the present Covenant recognize the right of everyone to the enjoyment of just and favourable conditions of work which ensure, in particular:

(a) Remuneration which provides all workers, as a minimum, with:

(i) Fair wages and equal remuneration for work of equal value without distinction of any kind, in particular women being guaranteed conditions of work not inferior to those enjoyed by men, with equal pay for equal work;

(ii) A decent living for themselves and their families in accordance with the provisions of the present Covenant;

(b) Safe and healthy working conditions;

(c) Equal opportunity for everyone to be promoted in his employment to an appropriate higher level, subject to no considerations other than those of seniority and competence;

(d) Rest, leisure and reasonable limitation of working hours and periodic holidays with pay, as well as remuneration for public holidays.[20]

In spite of the provisions of this core international human rights treaty, North Korea does nothing to ensure these rights, and in fact directly contravenes them at the expense of its people.

Additionally, the International Labour Organization's Protection of Wages Convention stipulates that wages should generally be paid directly in legal tender.[21] The Protection of Wages Convention gives some leeway to governments to apply provisions within the limits of "national laws and regulations," and Article 4 does allow for partial payment of wages in the form of allowances. However, it stipulates that these allowances should be "fair and reasonable" and that "such allowances are appropriate for the use and benefit of the worker and his family." North Korea's unwillingness to protect wages against steep deductions that limit the freedom of its workers is the clearest pattern that emerges from an analysis of North Korea's international labor practices. Wage violations affecting overseas workers are rampant. Workers are not paid directly by the foreign employers.[22]

---

[20] ICESCR, Article 7, http://www.ohchr.org/EN/ProfessionalInterest/Pages/CESCR.aspx.
[21] "C95 Protection of Wages Convention." International Labour Organization, http://www.ilo.org/dyn/normlex/en/f?p=NORMLEXPUB:12100:0::NO::P12100_ILO_COD E:C095. See also, International Labour Organization Convention No. 29 concerning Forced or Compulsory Labour; Convention No. 105 concerning the Abolition of Forced Labour; Convention No. 87 concerning Freedom of Association and Protection of the Right to Organise; Convention No. 98 concerning the Application of the Principles of the Right to Organise and to Bargain Collectively; Convention No. 100 concerning Equal Remuneration for Men and Women Workers for Work of Equal Value; Convention No. 111 concerning Discrimination in Respect of Employment and Occupation; Convention No. 138 concerning Minimum Age for Admission to Employment; Convention No. 182 concerning the Prohibition and Immediate Action for the Elimination of the Worst Forms of Child Labour.
[22] HRNK's findings on this topic concur with those of the Asan Institute of Policy Studies and the Database Center for North Korean Human Rights.

A former construction worker in the Middle East told HRNK: "We were slaves. [...] Bangladeshi workers doing similar work got paid 450 dollars a month on average. We also did earn the same amount, but it just all went to the Worker's Party... [...] But our families at home are still waiting in the hope of getting at least one TV when the fathers come back."

Another witness said:

"The system is so strict that no one in North Korea can ever criticize Kim Jong-il. That is why we continued working unpaid even after five months passed. The managerial staff would tell us, 'Back in our homeland people are starving and participating in the *Arduous March*.[23] We are blessed by the General to be out here and have white rice and beef soup every day. We should thank him for everything we have here.' That was our life at the construction site in the Middle East."[24]

Overtime violations are so egregious that the workers simply don't understand the concept. While overseas, North Koreans work between 14 and 16 hours a day, with no holidays, except perhaps one day a month, depending on location and industry:

"My morning shift was from 7am to 12pm. I had a lunch break from 12pm to 1pm. My evening shift was from 1pm to 6pm, and then I had a dinner break from 6pm to 7pm. After that I worked for three to four hours more. So it was 13 to 14 hours in total. There were no holidays."[25]

The overtime violations may be slightly less severe, if the workers have more specialized skills. A former construction welder in Russia told HRNK that he could leave earlier than other North Koreans, at about 7 or 8 pm. However, his life was harder than that of Russian co-workers. While he reported for work at 6 am, they did not show up until 9 am. They all got off by 5 pm, two or three hours before he did.

The evidence in every nation listed above indicates that North Korean workers abroad face steep and unfair deductions from their wages. The workers do not receive the full income directly and anecdotal evidence, defector testimonies, and government investigations indicate that the partial amount that the workers receive, no higher than 20% of the total, does not constitute a "fair and reasonable" allowance pursuant to Article 4, (2)(b) of the Protection of Wages Convention.

Forced Labor

While it is true that the information from the countries above strongly suggests that many of the workers were personally attracted to work overseas by the possibility of improving socioeconomic status in North Korea, or the relative misery of the situation within North Korea itself, this does not mean that North Korea's overseas workers are not victims of forced labor. Despite the fact that neither the ICCPR nor the ILO specific definition of forced labor fits the North Korean situation, forced labor may not necessarily mean that a worker was initially forced into employment. It may mean that the work environment is coercive and the employer/government prevents the worker from leaving on his/her own terms. If this is the definition of forced labor, coupled with the reality of 14-16 hour days with no time off, North Korea's workers abroad are victims of forced labor.

---

[23] Euphemism used by Kim regime propaganda to describe the great famine of the 1990s.
[24] HRNK interview with former construction worker in the Middle East. July 2013.
[25] Ibid.

Furthermore, the ICESCR speaks of the right to work as involving "productive employment under conditions safeguarding fundamental political and economic freedoms to the individual" (Art 6 (2)) and which provides for unions (Art 8).[26] In every situation, the North Korean government provides minders, ideology sessions, and barriers (even physical ones, as seen in Kuwait) to associating with other individuals and groups or leaving employment. Freedom of association is a fundamental labor right. It is clear that North Korean workers abroad do not have this essential freedom, much less the right to organize or bargain collectively for better terms.

When emergencies take place in foreign countries, North Korean workers are abandoned. This was the case of hundreds of North Korean workers who were left in Libya, once the 2011 civil war began. The North Korean government made no attempt to repatriate them. It is not clear whether that happened due to the lack of resources, inability to make logistical and transportation arrangements, or fear that they may bring back home their eyewitness account of the "Arab spring."

Future Direction: The Global Supply Chain

The term "global supply chain" aptly identifies both the challenges and opportunities inherent in handling North Korea's international economic outreach. North Korea's international labor force encompasses tens thousands of workers in many different countries and involves many businesses and consumers.

This new global outreach means that Pyongyang can no longer play solely on its own terms. North Korea may not be a party to most agreements governing human rights and labor, but the North Korean government is dealing with an increasingly globalized world in which all of the countries that employ North Korean workers are highly enmeshed in a body of international organizations and law setting forth standards for worker treatment.

As a country participating in this global supply chain, North Korea has opened itself up to additional recommendations to improve its labor standards. For example, in 2014, the UN Human Rights Council's Universal Periodic Review was conducted for the second time on North Korea's human rights record. States made recommendations to North Korea on labor and migrants issues, including:

- Consider acceding to the International Convention on the Elimination of All Forms of Racial Discrimination (ICERD) and the International Convention on the Protection of the Rights of All Migrant Workers and Members of Their Families (ICRMW) (Egypt);
- Ratify international conventions, particularly ICERD, CAT, ICRMW and the International Convention for the Protection of All Persons from Enforced Disappearance (CPED), with the aim of enacting them into national law (Sierra Leone);
- Consider promptly joining the International Labour Organization (Uruguay); and
- Take practical measures to provide safer working conditions, suitable for its citizens (Nicaragua).

Previously, in Cycle 1 of the UPR, these recommendations were made to North Korea:

- Amend the Labour Law of the Industrial Complex of Kaesong and incorporate the minimum age of 18 years for work hazardous to the health, security or morality of minors (Spain);
- Consider joining ILO and accede to and implement its core conventions, in particular Nos. 29, 105 and 182, on child and forced labour (Brazil);

---

[26] ICESCR, *supra* note 20.

- Consider signing-ratifying the remaining international human rights instruments, including ICERD and ICRMW (Nigeria);
- Invest sufficient resources to promote and protect the principle of equality in the fields of work, education and health (Libya);
- Join ILO and accede to its core instruments and extend an open invitation, and without restrictions, to ILO officials to analyze the situation of workers' rights in the country (Spain);
- Join ILO and ratify core conventions, particularly Nos. 105, 182 and 138, and allow related monitoring by ILO staff (United States);
- Put an end to forced labour practices (Chile, Cycles 1 and 2); and
- Take effective measures against the practice of forced labour, including child labour and join ILO (Italy).

A common theme throughout is for North Korea to join the ILO and implement better safety standards for its workers abroad.

External to the UN system, at times, NGOs may be tactically more effective, because there may be no need to target North Korea directly. Pressuring host countries that are more accountable than North Korea under international law and more exposed to the international economic system, and thus more vulnerable, may make the odds to facilitate real change more reasonable

In practice, NGOs can trace goods and services in the global supply chain to North Korean workers abroad. Simon Ostrovsky's article in *The Independent* on North Korean workers in Mongolia traced products from UK clothing labels such as Edinburgh Woolen Mill to North Korean workers.[27] Furthermore, it has been rumored that Land's End labels that say "Made in China" were really made by North Koreans in Rason. Supply chains depend on global consumption, and NGOs may effectively reduce demand for goods and services produced by North Korean workers if their work conditions continue to violate international standards. NGOs can also influence corporations to adhere to the Global Sullivan Principles and to only conduct business in countries that adhere to ILO standards, thus helping to regulate, oversee, and ensure that North Korean workers are not as vulnerable and exploitable.

Efforts aiming to improve the labor rights of overseas North Korean workers could target governments, employers' associations, companies, labor unions, NGOs, consumer groups, media organizations, and the general public in countries hosting North Korean workers, and could also aim to present a persuasive case to the North Korean authorities that improving the labor conditions of these workers may ultimately be in the best economic interest of North Korea. Most recently, the Construction Development Company in Qatar fired half its North Korean workers because of the violation of labor rights by the North Korean authorities.[28]

Despite the great difficulty in finding information on North Korea's international economic activity, let alone the status of its workers, by now there is sufficient evidence to argue that goods and services produced by North Korean workers abroad do not constitute part of a "clean" supply chain. Further, since

---

[27] Ostrovsky, Simon. "Profit from Its People: North Korea's Export Shame." The Independent, http://www.independent.co.uk/news/world/asia/profit-from-its-people-north-koreas-export-shame-2370220.html.

[28] Cho, Eunjung. "Qatari Firm Fires North Koreans, Cites Labor Exploitation." Voice of America exclusive report. May 7, 2015. http://www.voanews.com/content/exclusive-qatari-firm-fires-north-koreans-citing-labor-exploitation/2753359.html.

supply chains that produce clothes or industrial goods are typically international, it is perfectly legitimate to use the conventions of the International Labour Organization as a standard for a clean supply chain. The ILO does not have to deal with North Korea directly; it can evaluate and publicize the situation of North Korean workers in its 183 member states.

Recommendations to the U.S. Congress

To improve the working conditions and human rights of North Korean workers officially residing overseas, the following recommendations are offered:

First, the U.S. Congress should devise a strategy that addresses the issues of North Korean human rights and labor violations that impact the American economy, to include periodically holding hearings on this topic in order to hear from stakeholders and inform the public. As such, North Korea should be urged to abide by its legal obligations under the ICCPR and the ICESCR and its own domestic legislation to protect the rights of its workers, at home and abroad.

Second, the U.S. Congress should make clear that U.S. companies doing business with North Korean companies or workers that are violating labor and human rights laws must operate under a set of standards inspired by the Global Sullivan Principles or terminate their relationship. Companies along the supply chain tainted by violations of the rights of exported North Korean workers should be encouraged to apply those standards.

Third, the U.S. Congress should collaborate with the Department of State to ensure that the Trafficking in Persons Report further investigates the situation of exported North Korean laborers.

Fourth, the U.S. should continue to support NGOs tasked to monitor the severe labor and human rights violations occurring at worksites with overseas North Korean workers so that their work can inform the American public and American corporations conducting business in host countries. Likewise, a Congressional Research Service report on these issues should be conducted.

Fifth, the U.S. should continue to recommend that North Korea join the ILO and ratify its core conventions, particularly Nos. 105, 182, and 138, and allow related monitoring by ILO staff. As previously mentioned, states have made these recommendations to North Korea during its UPR. North Korea's response, however, has primarily been to "note" the recommendations, not accept or reject them. Encouragingly, perhaps, North Korea "accepted" Nicaragua's recommendation to "Take practical measures to provide safer working conditions, suitable for its citizens." This should be pressed well in advance of North Korea's next UPR in 2019.

Sixth, the U.S. Congress should collaborate with the U.S. Ambassador to the UN to request that she advocate that:

- at the 25th Anniversary of the ICRMW on December 18, 2015, the Committee on Migrant Workers[29] remind countries with North Korean laborers to abide by their international

---

[29] Members are from the following states: Philippines, Ecuador, Honduras, Argentina, Mali, Egypt, Morocco, Bangladesh, Sri Lanka, Algeria, Peru, Burkina Faso, Azerbaijan, and Senegal. *See* http://www.ohchr.org/EN/HRBodies/CMW/Pages/Membership.aspx.

obligations and take steps to protect the rights of all foreign workers, including North Korean workers, in particular for those whose wages and working hours rights are violated;

- the UN Committee on Migrant Workers push for an investigation on North Korean workers overseas in countries that are states parties to the ICRMW;
- the UN Special Rapporteur on Contemporary form of Slavery and the UN Special Rapporteur on the situation of human rights in the DPRK further investigate the situation of exported North Korean laborers, and the cooperation of host countries should be sought;
- North Korea accede to or sign the International Convention on the Protection of the Rights of All Migrant Workers and Members of their Families.[30]

Furthermore, Congress should request that the U.S. Ambassador to the UN meet with the UN Committee on Migrant Workers to push for an investigation on North Korean workers overseas in countries that are states parties to the ICRMW.

Additionally, the U.S. Ambassador to the UN should urge the UN Economic and Social Commission for Asia and the Pacific (ESCAP), which trains North Koreans in business management and law, to include in that training material and guidance on the UN Global Compact's principles for companies, specifying labor standards and workers' rights.[31]

Seventh, violations of the labor rights of North Korean workers residing overseas should be included in future legislation pertaining to sanction regimes. As such, Congress should pass the North Korea Sanctions Enforcement Act of 2015 (H.R. 757),[32] which allows for sanctions against persons (or entities) "knowingly engaging in or contributing to activities in North Korea, through export or import, which involve"..."human rights abuses."[33]

Eighth, the U.S. should ban the import of products made by North Korean migrant workers, if produced in violation of international labor and human rights laws.[34]

For the State Department

Ninth, host countries should be persuaded by the relevant U.S. Country Team to conduct both scheduled and surprise inspections of worksites employing North Korean workers, pursuant to their international obligations.

Tenth, a determination should be made by the relevant U.S. Country Team and by the Special Rapporteur on human rights in the DPRK if the presence of tens of thousands of North Korean citizens overseas may

---

[30] ICRMW, 18 December 1990, http://www.ohchr.org/EN/ProfessionalInterest/Pages/CMW.aspx.

[31] Roberta Cohen, *Must UN Agencies Also Fail in North Korea?*, 21 April 2015, 38 North, USKI-SAIS, http://38north.org/2015/04/rcohen042115/. See also ESCAP, *NGOs and the Private Sector*, http://www.unescap.org/partners/working-with-escap/ngos-and-the-private-sector. The ROK is a major donor to ESCAP. http://www.unescap.org/partners/working-with-escap/donors

[32] Library of Congress, *Summaries for the North Korea Sanctions Enforcement Act of 2015*, https://www.govtrack.us/congress/bills/114/hr757/summary.

[33] *Id.*

[34] As recommended by PSCORE; *see* A/HRC/28/NGO/51, 20 February 2015, http://ap.ohchr.org/documents/dpage_e.aspx?c=50&su=59.

provide opportunities for access to improve the human rights situation of North Koreans at home and abroad, despite their being subjected to draconian control and surveillance by the North Korean authorities.

Eleventh, hosting states and employers should be encouraged by the relevant U.S. Country Team to seek direct access to North Korean workers and distribute material informing them of their rights derived from their physical presence within the territorial jurisdiction of that respective country.

Other Recommendations

Twelfth, the eight ILO Core conventions on fundamental labor standards should be the minimum standard applied to determine the status of exported North Korean workers and to hold both North Korea and receiving countries accountable.

Thirteenth, the exportation of North Korean labor should be terminated through concerted international action, if the North Korean regime refuses to act upon calls to improve the working conditions and the overall human rights situation of these workers.

Thank you, Chairman Pitts. I look forward to answering any questions you might have.

MR.PITTS. The chair thanks the gentleman.

Mr. Lim IL, you are recognized for your opening statement.

STATEMENT OF MR. IL

MR.IL. [The following testimony was delivered through an interpreter.] It is my honor to testify in front of the Tom Lantos Human Rights Committee today to share my story as an overseas worker.

I was born in October of 1968 in Pyongyang, North Korea. My life as an overseas worker, which was then and still is one of the most prestigious job in North Korea, started in early September of 1996 with a training class on how to propagate the Kim Jung Il and North Korean system in other countries.

The company I worked for is an independent construction company which was supervised by Pyongyang Foreign Construction Enterprise. There were 600 North Korean workers like me at the time. There were two other North Korean companies similar to mine, so for a total more than 1,100 North Korean workers were employed. The dormitory for North Korean workers was a closed school due to the bombing during the Gulf War. The classrooms were used as the rooms for sleep and the gym was used for a cafeteria and a meeting room. The portraits of Kim Il Sung and Kim Jung Il was hung in every schoolroom and the slogan of the Workers Party of North Korea was hung in the middle room.

As soon as I arrived in Kuwait, I started to work from 7:00 a.m. to 7:00 p.m. every day at this housing construction site. I worked as a carpenter assembling timber work. The lunch break was an hour, from 12:00 p.m. to 1:00 p.m. Because of the weather in Kuwait, the local workers had three hours of lunch time while the North Korean workers had one hour. Dinner started at 8:00 p.m. and we were allowed to take a shower and have free time in the evening. After dinner, the propaganda education class follows including so-called evaluation time when we were surveyed. From 10:00 p.m. we are allowed to go to bed. However, once -- in three days we were required to do extra work at night. The North Korean officials always said let us finish the construction as soon as possible so we can give joy to our supreme leader, Kim Jong Il. No one could say no to this because if one did so he or she was considered as a reactionary and repatriated to North Korea. So it was normal for us to work 14 hours a day. We could have a day off on Friday twice in the month. We usually spent that time doing laundry, sleep, play card games and talk about our home town in North Korea. However, we never talked about the politics such as the North Korean regime or the supreme leader. Even during the day off we were allowed to go to the off site dormitory. North Korean officials often said that the South Korean agents can kidnap you anytime if you go out. So you can just stay only inside the dormitory.

Five months later, I realized that I have never been paid at all while I was working in Kuwait. When I was asked about my salary, the work officials said that the company in Kuwait was experiencing economic difficulty. The second time I asked, the official said that the Workers Party did not command to pay us yet. No one could raise questions since then because in North Korea the Workers Party meant the supreme leader and was not allowed to complain about whatever the party decided. Then I met another North Korean worker who had worked there for a year and he told me that he had not been paid for the whole time. I realized that I was dispatched to Kuwait not to earn money but just to eat and work. It was very clear that there was no hope in North Korea, my home country.

In March 1997, I went to the South Korean embassy in Kuwait in order to go to South Korea. At the embassy, I said, "I hate North Korea, where I lived for my entire life." Even though I was dispatched to North Korea, I was continuously brainwashed by the North Korean authorities on Kim Jong Il and forced to monitor my fellow North Korean workers and I haven't been paid at all. I went to live in South Korea. I don't know much about South Korea but I am sure that it will not be like North Korea. I sat in the South Korean embassy for five days and while I was there I found out that based on the contract the company in Kuwait paid $550 per month for each worker to the North Korean company. Therefore, my salary, which I never received, went directly to Office Number 39 of Workers Party, which manages foreign currency.

In North Korea, Kim Jong Un needs millions of dollars only to maintain his political power. It costs $200 million dollars a year to manage Kumsusan Palace where the corpse of Kim Il Sung and Kim Jung Il are preserved. Also, Kim Jong Un constantly offers presents such as luxurious cars, apartments, household appliances to the Workers Party officials in order to keep them loyal to him. Furthermore, Kim needs foreign currency to maintain his own luxurious life. He has more than 20 luxurious villas all around North Korea and they cost $300 million to just maintain those villas. Last year, he spent $640 million to buy his own luxurious items and fine cuisine. That is why the North Korean overseas laborers like me are continuously sent to earn foreign currency in order to keep the luxurious lifestyle of Kim Jong Un and his followers.

There are still about 4,600 North Korean workers in Kuwait and at least 50,000 North Korean workers in 40 different countries who raise $1.2 billion to $2.3 billion each year. They are forced to do slave labor like me where they work for more than 14 hours a day without receiving any salary. Still my co-workers in Kuwait appear in my dream and ask, did you go to Seoul only for your own survival -- please expose our miserable experience to the world. They never have known about the universal rights for human beings but they are the same human beings like us.

I sincerely ask you to have a deep concern in North Korean overseas workers who are still doing the forced slave labors.
Thank you.

MR.PITTS. The chair thanks the gentleman very much for his testimony.
I now recognize Mr. John Sifton for your opening statement.

[The statement of Mr. Il follows:]

My Life as a North Korean Overseas Worker in Kuwait
Lim Il, Former North Korean Overseas Worker in Kuwait

I was born in October 1968 in Pyongyang, North Korea. After graduating from high school, I worked in Social Safety Agency and Foreign Construction Complex for 12 years in North Korea. In early September 1996 in Pyongyang, I was selected to be an overseas worker. After being selected, I was trained by the Workers' Party, which is the sole governing party of North Korea. The North Korean authorities taught me how to propagate Kim Jong Il and the North Korean system in other countries.

In Kuwait, I belonged to Liberation Construction Company of North Korea, which was organized by Pyongyang Foreign Construction Complex. There were about 600 North Korean workers like me. At that time, there were 3 companies of North Korea like mine in Kuwait.

One was a construction company which was established by the General Bureau of Capital Construction of North Korea with 700 North Korean workers dispatched. The other one was a construction company which was established by the General Bureau of Neungra Construction of North Korea with 500 North Korean workers dispatched.

The North Korean dormitory where I was stayed in Kuwait was a closed school which was bombed in the Gulf War in 1991. The class rooms were used as rooms for sleep, and the gym was used for a cafeteria and a meeting room. The portraits of Kim Il Sung and Kim Jong Il were hung in every class room. The slogan of the Workers' Party of North Korea was hung in the meeting room.
On November 8, 1996, the day after I arrived in Kuwait, I woke up at 5A.M. and ate breakfast at 6A.M. The North Korean authorities in Kuwait provided 200g of bread, a cup of coffee, butter and an egg as a breakfast. Compared to breakfast in Pyongyang, it was fairly good.

In the morning, I worked from 7A.M. to 12P.M. I worked in a housing construction site in a huge, empty desert. Based on the architectural drawing, I assembled timberwork for throwing cement. I was a carpentry worker.

The lunch time was from 12P.M. to 1P.M. The North Korean authorities provided rice, beef soup and kimchi as lunch. Because of the weather in Kuwait, the local workers had 3 hours of lunch time while North Korean workers had one hour of lunch time.

After lunch, I started to work again from 1P.M. Around 4P.M. the workers from other countries received snacks (bread, milk, and coke) from the Kuwait company, but the North Korean workers did not receive any. The workers from other countries asked us why we do not receive any snack. Then some of the North Korean workers answered, "We, North Korean workers, do not like snacks. Instead, we are trained by the North Korean authorities about revolution." However, the North Korean workers were not happy saying that.

The work finished at 7P.M., and from then the workers ate dinner by 8P.M. Every North Korean worker wanted to eat dinner and sleep, but the reality was not like that. The dinner menu was always same as lunch menu. Sometimes, the North Korean authorities provided noodle as dinner to save money.
You would not believe it but in North Korea, only high officials of the Workers' Party can eat bread, egg, beef soup, and noodle for every meal. General citizens in North Korea cannot even imagine to eat them. So, the North Korean authorities in Kuwait emphasized that what we, the North Korean workers dispatched to Kuwait, eat is sumptuous food so we have to appreciate it. Since the authorities said so, we had to appreciate the small amount of meal.

From 8P.M. the North Korean workers and I were allowed to take shower and have cultural life. In the dormitory, there was a shower facility, but the water was provided only for an hour. The North Korean authorities did so to save money.

After taking shower, the North Korean workers and I had to be trained by the North Korean authorities. Even in Kuwait, the North Korean workers and I had to have evaluation time every Saturday, take education on the Supreme Leader every Wednesday, and take a lecture on policies of the Workers' Party every Friday. In the meeting room, every North Korean worker had to watch the documentary on Kim Jong Il. On Kim Jong Il's birthday on February 16, every North Korean worker had to confirm and show our loyalty to Kim Jong Il.

At 10P.M., I was allowed to sleep. However, every one day in three days, I had to do the night work. The North Korean officials at the work site forced me to do the night work by saying, "Let's finish the construction as soon as possible so that we can give joy to our Supreme Leader Kim Jong Il." No North Korean workers can say "No" to this. If one does so, he or she is considered as a reactionary and is repatriated to North Korea.

Every North Korean worker should obey what the North Korean officials said, so we did the night work from 9P.M. to 12A.M. Even though we over worked, the North Korean officials did not pay us for it. Therefore, we worked almost 11 hours a day, and including the night work, we worked 14 hours a day. We only had a holiday on Friday of the second week and the fourth week of a month. During holiday, we did laundry, slept, played card game, and talked about our hometown in North Korea. However, we never talked about politics such as the North Korean government, Supreme Leader, etc.

Based on the rule of North Korea, the North Korean overseas workers are not allowed to go outside of the work site of the dormitory. Particularly, an individual action is not allowed. The North Korean officials brainwashed us by saying, "The South Korean agents can kidnap you at any time if you go out of the dormitory so you should stay only in the dormitory."

If someone has to go outside, he or she has to go with more than 2 other people and tell what they did outside to the North Korea officials. This is the rule for all North Korean overseas workers. Also, the North Korean overseas workers have to watch each other. I also did.

However, the North Korean authorities did not pay me at all while I was working in Kuwait. When I asked about my salary, the North Korean officials said that the contracted company in Kuwait is having an economic difficulty so they cannot pay me. The second time I asked about my salary, the North Korean officials said that the Workers' Party of North Korea did not command them to pay us. For it, no one could raise questions any more. In North Korea, the Workers' Party means the Supreme Leader, so no one can raise any complaint against it.

At the work site in Kuwait, I met another North Korean worker who worked there for one year, and he told me that he and other North Korean workers did not get paid for a year. After hearing about that, I was in despair. I realized that I was dispatched to Kuwait not to earn money but just to eat and work. Even though I worked very hard, I was not compensated at all.

I thought many times but did not get any solution for it. It was a pain to be brainwashed about Kim Il Sung and Kim Jong Il's ideologies even in Kuwait. We had to be evaluated for our ideologies every week and watch each other even in Kuwait. So I realized that there is no hope in North Korea, my home country. In March 1997, I went to the South Korean Embassy in Kuwait to go to South Korea. At the Embassy, I said, "I hate North Korea, where I lived for my entire life. Even though I was dispatched to Kuwait, I was continuously brainwashed by the North Korean authorities on Kim Jong Il's ideologies and was forced to watch my fellow North Korean workers. Also, I was not paid at all. I want to live in South Korea. I don't know well about South Korea but I'm sure it would not like North Korea."

I legally entered Kuwait so I went to UNHCR in Kuwait to be accepted as a refugee. I stayed in the South Korean Embassy for five days, and while I was staying here, I came to know that the company in Kuwait which made a contract with North Korea regularly gave salaries for the North Korean workers ($550 per one North Korean worker) to the North Korean company. Therefore, my salaries, which I never received, went to the North Korean authorities, which is No.39 Office of the Workers' Party which manages foreign currency.

In North Korea, the Leader Kim Jong Un needs a huge amount of money to maintain his regime. First, it costs 200 million dollars a year to manage the Palace where the corps of Kim Il Sung and Kim Jong Il are preserved. The regime will keep maintaining the Palace because it can effectively control people in North Korea by idolizing the dead supreme leaders.

Furthermore, Kim Jong Un should constantly offer presents such as luxurious cars, apartments and household appliances to the officials of the Workers' Party in order to make them be loyal to him. To buy such luxurious presents to maintain his regime, Kim Jong Un needs huge amount of foreign currency. Another reason why Kim Jong Un needs foreign currency is to maintain his own luxurious life. He has more than 20 luxurious villas in North Korea, and it costs 300 million dollars to maintain those villas. Last year, he spent 640 million dollars to buy his own luxurious items and fine cuisine.
Enormous amount of money has been spent for Kim Jong Un's own pleasure. Therefore, the North Korean overseas laborers like me should earn foreign currency because their leader said so, and the money that they earn constantly goes to the regime.

In North Korea, it is strictly forbidden to talk about Kim Jong Un's private life.
Nobody tries to know about it. If someone does, he or she would be considered as a reactionary and severely punished. The regime actually removes such person from the society. If someone is just suspected

to criticize Kim Jong Un, he or she would suddenly disappear someday. This is very common in North Korea.

North Korea exists only for Kim Jong Un, the dictator. Half of the people in North Korea barely survive by eating grass soup, but the regime always blames USA and South Korea for their poverty. I don't know whether the supreme leader, Kim Jong Un, knows the reality of the people or not, but what I know is that he doesn't care about it at all.

There are still 20,000 workers in Kuwait, where I used to work. The work site where I used to work is another North Korea in Kuwait. I was forced to do slave labor there with many other North Korean workers dispatched. We had to work for more than 14 hours a day without receiving any salary.

To be honest with you, my co-workers in Kuwait still appear in my dream and say to me, "Did you go to Seoul only for your survival? Please expose our miserable lives to the world." They don't know about the universal rights for human being but they are the same human beings like us. I sincerely ask you to have a deep concern in the North Korean overseas workers who are still doing the forced slave labors.

Thank you.

STATEMENT OF MR. SIFTON

MR.SIFTON. Thank you, Mr. Chairman, for inviting me to testify today on this important subject.

The other witnesses have already provided details on how North Korea forces its citizens into abusive work overseas and then pockets most of their compensation. I would like to use my time to offer some other more general observations about the phenomenon and the context in which it occurs.

First off, I wanted to note that the phenomenon is complex. There is no one single model for what is going on with North Koreans working outside of North Korea. Our research, as well as our colleagues', show that workers are being used in many different countries across the world -- China, Eastern Europe, the Middle East, Russia and in Southeast Asia. There were even for a time restaurants with North Korean workers in Australia and the Netherlands. Workers are involved in a bevy of different types of work -- heavy labor, logging and factory work -- but we also know that they toil in restaurants as wait staff and performers, bussing tables or rehearsing and then singing and dancing for tourists, in addition to their wait staff. These are mostly -- the tourists are mostly South Koreans who give generous tips when staff sings songs, generous tips which are not, of course, transferred to workers.

We also know that in almost all these cases, whether wait staff or loggers or what have you, the workers' lack of liberty meets the international legal definition of trafficking. We also know that the specifics of these business operations can vary. In some cases, governments pay the North Korean government directly for the use of North Korean labor in state-owned enterprises. In other cases, local businesses -- business owners in a country pay money to the North Korean government directly. Sometimes, however, wages are given to North Korean government offices who then supposedly pay workers. Other times a third party company receives the wages, hands over most of the compensation to the North Korean government. Whatever the specifics, in most cases, as Ambassador King mentioned and my colleagues have mentioned, workers receive only a small portion of the supposed compensation, if that. They are paid in bulk at the end of their work, usually three years. They may be given small stipends for personal use but nothing approaching compensation.

In some cases, as my colleague mentioned, workers are allowed to seek additional irregular work on local businesses when their regular work is interrupted, such as in China where logging operations using North Korean workers may be curtailed in the summer because of rain and mud. These workers go and seek work in farms and other businesses. But in those cases as well, they have to hand over most of their wages to their handlers. In other cases, however, with waitresses, for instance, they are obliged to stay in their compound, only working in that restaurant. The waitresses occasionally can leave to go to markets but they must go in pairs, and it is worth remarking that many, after a long day of rehearsing their dance and song routines and then bussing tables, serving food, then have to sit down at the end of the day and write out essentially a self-denunciation in which they report on what all the South Korean tourists have asked them about during the day and how they responded and what they said, and that is part of their work as well. Anyway, the bottom line is that there is no single manifestation of the use of forced labor. We shouldn't simplify it into a single type of work. Different things are going on in different places.

The second point I wanted to make is there is a larger context which you made yourself in the opening statement and Ambassador King noted. There is no doubt that these workers are subjected to serious human rights abuses. They meet the definition of human trafficking. Their liberty, their right of compensation for work are being violated, among many other abuses. But as you mentioned, Mr. Chairman, in a perverse demonstration of how abusive North Korea is, some of these workers are nonetheless among the most fortunate or more fortunate of North Korean citizens in that they are allowed to travel abroad and work.

Inside North Korea, making money, even at very low wages, is very difficult and especially when citizens are already obligated to work with the state at almost impossibly low wages. Many, in addition to their regular work, are routinely forced to carry out unpaid work for government projects. Forced labor is endemic inside of North Korea. Students, for instance, are required to leave school to plant rice in the spring, harvest it in the fall. Workers are obligated to meet quotas for scavenging scrap metal or stones and pebbles for road work.

As my colleague mentioned, some of the workers outside of North Korea, even the loggers and the construction workers, are being selected from the highest strata of the songbun system -- the higher up system under which North Korea lives. Not the highest levels but among the higher loyal classes. We also need to remember that there are workers at the Kaesong Industrial Complex. Now, it is inside of North Korea but they are working for South Korean industries for wages that are believed to be largely pocketed by the North Korean government.

Third, the last main point I wanted to make there is another rights issue to mention, which has been alluded to already -- the revenue stream to Pyongyang. But the issue is a little bit complex. There is no doubt that these -- that these abuses, this system, provides a revenue stream to the North Korean government and the military in particular which is, after all, the biggest consumer of government revenue. It is tempting to look at the issue of forced labor from a prohibition standpoint. These abuses are terrible. We should do everything we can to shut the system down, send these workers home, cut off this revenue stream. This may not be the most strategic approach. We don't want to come down hard on either way but I think it needs some more discussion about whether that is the right approach.

First, it needs to be recognized that the United States government in particular and its allies have a sharply limited ability to curtail this system, especially since most of this work is being done in Russia and China. The system is going to continue as it is until there are major changes to the international sanctions regime as it applies to North Korea and those are the types of changes, given the current situation, that are not going to occur anytime soon. But if there are major events in North Korea that change the underlying political dynamics that might be possible.

The second -- some observers note that horrible as the system is -- it is abusive, it provides revenue to the North Korean government -- it also may be an Achilles Heel for the regime. Every worker who leaves North Korea is one more worker who can return home with knowledge of the world outside and this may, may, undermine the government's fictional narrative about the government's proper treatment of its population. In addition, there are major economic changes underway in North Korea. I wouldn't call it open -- an opening market, but individuals are undertaking more private enterprises -- selling items, offering services -- and it may be that some of those overseas wages remitted home, small as they are, are feeding that growth. Maybe. Even if the North Korean government takes $4 out of every $5 made by workers outside, the $1 left is still a dollar that returns to North Korea and perhaps, maybe, is part of this newer non-state economy and the possibilities that creates for greater openness in the long term should be considered at least.

Third, we don't know really how much revenue the system provides to the government. We have estimates. But they need to be compared to the other revenue streams that Pyongyang is getting from other things like weapon sales and smuggling and other illicit criminal activities. With more information about that we can decide whether this issue should be approached from a sanctions perspective or maybe instead from a labor rights perspective.

I am going to end by talking about that. What would it mean to focus on this overseas labor not from a sanctioning point of view, which may be the right thing to do. But putting that to the side, what would it mean to focus instead on a labor rights perspective? Well, mainly, it means exploring whether it is possible to compel authorities in some of the countries where the work is occurring to undertake better monitoring and enforcement of labor provisions, difficult as that may be. The International Labor Organization, for instance, works in some of these countries where workers are found -- Burma, Cambodia, Malaysia, Mongolia.

Could these offices be asked to get involved in visiting workplaces, offering counseling for workers? Would this lead perhaps to employers being forced to allow these workers some more freedoms? Could it encourage some of these workers to stand up to abuses or even seek refuge abroad? Could it lead to workers returning to North Korea with a better understanding of just how abusive their government is? Would it allow the workers to obtain more of their compensation? It is possible. These approaches are worth exploring. Exposure, monitoring, counseling could lead, in some cases, to some mitigation of the worst forms of these abuses.

We would basically like to make the following recommendations of the committee and members of Congress who are concerned. Pressing the State Department to exercise more pressure on the countries with workplaces with North Korean workers to inspect and monitor those workplaces and facilitate outside counseling to the workers about their rights. This may not be possible in Russia or China but it definitely is possible in Phnom Penh and Kuala Lumpur and wherever else in Southeast Asia these workers can be found. Request the State Department and USAID to explore with other donors how they can strengthen the ILO and other labor organizations and groups as well as local government agencies in the countries like the ones I just mentioned to better monitor workplaces that use North Korean workers and offer counseling. Third, request that the U.S. trade representative report to Congress on whether provisions are being included or can be added to the Trans-Pacific Partnership to obligate partners in that agreement to improve their labor monitoring and inspection capabilities. That is worth mentioning, of course, that Vietnam and Malaysia are potential members of the Trans-Pacific Partnership and these are places where North Korean workers have been found at times. And last, I mean, request the administration to provide better information on the estimates of the revenue generated by the North Korean government from overseas labor and to compare it with other revenue streams because I feel like that intelligence, that information, would be very useful in deciding what the proper approaches to this problem are.

I would be glad to answer any more questions. Thank you for allowing me to testify.

[The statement of Mr. Sifton follows:]

Thank you for inviting me to testify today on this important subject. The issue of North Koreans being subjected to forced labor outside of their country is a timely topic. The other witnesses on the panel have provided key details on exactly how North Korea forces its citizens into abusive work environments outside their country and then takes most of the compensation produced by this labor. I would like to use my time to offer some more general observations about this pervasive phenomenon and the context in which it occurs.

1. *The phenomenon is complex.* There is no single model for what's going on with respect to the use of forced labor by North Koreans outside North Korea. Based on our research and review of accounts collected by other research groups and media, we know that North Korean workers are being used in numerous countries across the world, in China, in eastern Europe, the Middle East, Russia, Mongolia, Malaysia, Burma, Cambodia—there were even some for a time in Australia and the Netherlands. We know the workers are involved in heavy labor, logging, and factory work. But they also toil in restaurants as wait staff and performers, bussing tables, and rehearing, singing, and dancing for South Korean and other tourists. We know that in almost all cases, the workers' lack of liberty meets the international legal definition of trafficking.

    North Korea's export labor is managed by the government, but business operations vary widely. In some cases, a government or state-owned or state-controlled enterprise will pay the North Korean government directly for the use of North Korea labor. In other cases local business owners pay money to the North Korean government. In some cases, wages are given to North Korean government offices which then supposedly pay workers, in other cases a third-party company or North Korean company receives wages and hands over most of the compensation to the North Korean government . In most cases, workers receive only a small portion of the supposed compensation, they are paid in a cash bulk at the end of their stay, usually three years, and are given small stipends for personal use. In some cases, workers are allowed to seek additional irregular work on local businesses when their regular work is interrupted, as in Russia, where logging operations using North Korean workers are curtailed in rainy summer months due to muddy ground conditions. In other cases, as with waitresses, workers are obliged to stay on their compound, only working in one place. The bottom line is that there is no single manifestation of the use of forced labor and we should avoid simplifying it to a single type of work. Different things are going on in different places.

2. *There is a larger context: abuses in North Korea generally.* North Korea workers outside of North Korea are being subjected to serious human rights abuses. Their liberty and right to fair compensation for work are being violated, among other abuses. In a perverse demonstration of how abusive North Korea is—some of these workers are nonetheless among the more fortunate of North Korean citizens in being allowed to travel abroad and work. Inside North Korea, making money—even at very low wages—is exceedingly difficult, especially when many citizens are already obligated to work for the state at almost impossibly low wages and, in addition to any regular work, are routinely forced to undertake routine forced labor for special projects or needs. Forced labor is of course endemic inside North Korea as well: students, for instance, are required to leave school to plant rice in the spring, and harvest it in the fall. Workers throughout the country are obligated to spend time outside of work fulfilling quotas for scavenging for scrap metal or stones for road work. Some of the workers outside of North Korea, even loggers and construction workers, are being selected from among the higher stratas of North Korea's highly hierarchical Songbun system—not the highest, but close. And workers at the Kasong Industrial Complex inside of North Korea are working for South Korean industries for wages that are largely pocketed by the North Korean government.

All of these workers are victims, of course, of a totalitarian system. The entire citizenry, even many of the personnel who themselves enforce the abusive practices, are themselves victims of it. But it is important to understand the overseas forced labor abuses in context to the larger picture.

3. *There is a secondary rights issue: the revenue that the system provides to the Pyongyang government—but the issue is a complex one.* The human rights issues are not only about the abusive use of forced labor, but concern the larger fact that the abuses provide a revenue stream to the North Korean government and the military in particular, the biggest consumer of government revenue.

   It is tempting to look at the issue of forced labor from a prohibition perspective, and say "these abuses are terrible," and "we should do everything we can to shut this down, send these workers home, cut off this revenue stream to the abusive government." This may not be the most strategic approach, however.

   a. First, it should be recognized that the United States government and its allies have sharply limited ability to curtail this forced labor system, especially given that much of the work is being done in countries like Russia and China. The system is going to continue until there are major changes to the international sanctions regime as it applies to North Korea—and these are the kind of changes that, given the China and Russia veto in the Security Council, can only occur if major events in North Korea change underlying political dynamics.

   b. Second, some observers note that horrible as the system is—that it is abusive and provides revenue to the North Korean government—it also may be an Achilles Heel for the government. Every worker who leaves North Korea is one more worker who can return home with knowledge of the world outside, and undermine the government's fictional narrative about a government's proper treatment of its population. Major economic changes are underway in North Korea: individuals are undertaking more and more private enterprises—selling items, offering services—and it may be that some of the overseas wages remitted home, small as they are, are feeding that growth. Even if the North Korean government takes four dollars for every five dollars made by workers outside, the one dollar left that returns to North Korea is a dollar more that will filter into North Korea's newer non-state economy and the possibilities it creates for greater openness in the long term.

   c. Third, we don't really know how much revenue this system provides to the government. It would be better to learn more about how significant the revenue is from overseas forced labor before addressing it as a target for sanctions or prohibition. If Pyongyang's three top revenue streams come from other areas—say, weapons sales, smuggling, and other illicit criminal schemes—then it is those areas which deserve the most attention from the revenue perspective, while issues with overseas workers can be approached less from a sanctions perspective and more from a labor rights perspective.

   What does it mean to focus on overseas labor from a labor rights perspective? It would mean swallowing some of our outrage at the sheer abusiveness of the trafficking and compulsion of the system and exploring whether it might be possible to compel authorities in countries in which work is occurring to undertake monitoring and enforcement of labor provisions, difficult as they may be.

The International Labor Organization, for instance, works in some of these countries—Burma, Cambodia, Malaysia, Mongolia. Could their offices be asked to get involved in visiting workplaces and offering counseling for workers? Would this lead, perhaps, to employers being forced to allow those workers more freedoms? Could it encourage some of these workers to stand up to abuses or seek refuge abroad? Could it lead to workers, even if they remain in abusive situations, returning to North Korea with a better understanding of how abusive their government is, and spreading that understanding to others? Would it allow the workers to obtain more of their compensation?

These approaches are worth exploring. Exposure, monitoring, and counseling could lead in some cases to some mitigation of the worst forms of abuse or exploitation, and to other potentially positive outcomes. Countries which are part of the Trans-Pacific Partnership—Vietnam, Malaysia—could also be put on notice that it is expected that their improved labor rights protections under the agreement will oblige them to monitor and crack down on abusive labor arrangements on their territory, including those involving North Korean workers.

Recommendations

Human Rights Watch makes the following recommendations of the committee and to members of Congress concerned by the topic of the hearing today:

- Press the State Department to exercise more pressure on countries with workplaces with North Korean workers to inspect and monitor those workplaces, and facilitate counseling to workers about their rights.
- Request the State Department and USAID to explore with other donors how the ILO and other international labor organizations and groups, as well as local government agencies in receptive countries, can better monitor workplaces that use North Korean workers and offer counseling.
- Request that the US Trade Representative report to Congress on whether provisions are included or can be added to the Trans-Pacific Partnership to obligate partners in the agreement to improve their labor monitoring and inspection capacities, including for workplaces using North Korean workers.
- Request the administration to provide better information on estimates of the revenue generated by the North Korean government from overseas labor, in comparison with other revenue streams.

Thank you for inviting me to testify today.

MR.PITTS. The chair thanks the gentleman, thanks all the witnesses for your testimony and I will begin the questioning and recognize myself for that purpose.

We will begin with you, Mr. Scarlatoiu. Estimates of the number of North Koreans in government-run overseas labor programs we have heard range from 20,000 to 100,000. What estimate do you view as accurate? Aside from China and Russia, which countries are thought to have the large numbers of North Korean workers? You mentioned, I think, 16 countries.

MR. SCARLATOIU. Mr. Chairman, I estimate the 50,000 number to be most accurate. This is a number recently produced by the Osan Institute of Policy Studies in South Korea and also for the database center for North Korean human rights in South Korea.
Regarding the numbers in the particular countries, there are 20,000 in Russia, 19,000 in China, 1,300 in Mongolia, 5,000 in Kuwait, 2,000 in the United Arab Emirates, 1,800 in Qatar, 1,000 in Angola, 400 to 500 in Poland, 300 in Malaysia, 300 in Oman, 300 in Libya, 200 in Myanmar, 200 in Nigeria, 200 in Algeria, 200 in Equatorial Guinea and 100 in Ethiopia. With the exception of Algeria and Equatorial Guinea, all of these countries are ILO member states.

MR.PITTS. And the 19,000 was what country?

MR. SCARLATOIU. The 19,000 was in China. The number may be higher. This may just be a conservative estimate. It is probably better to err on that side.

MR. PITTS. Thank you. What are the mechanisms by which North Korean workers or their North Korean government agents transfer money back to the North Korean government?

MR. SCARLATOIU. There are cash transfers taking place, as mentioned earlier. Sometimes good that are coveted in North Korea are transferred, as Ambassador King mentioned earlier. One rather strange example is that of deer navel, which appears to be a sought after product in North Korea. I have received reports from former North Korean workers that this is one of the products that they bring back. All of them say that they never bring back large amounts of money. That is a red flag for the authorities and they may think that there is something else going on. The North Korean workers themselves and perhaps the authorities may have learned from migrant workers working side by side about Hawala-type systems of transferring money through underground channels to their countries of origin.

MR. PITTS. Finally, according to some analysts, conditions for some North Korean overseas workers are freer and more lucrative than for many workers inside North Korea. What evidence is there to support these observations?

MR. SCARLATOIU. The question is the degree to which they are allowed to seek opportunities. I think that this is a change that pertains to North Korea in general. After the great famine that ravaged North Korea in the 1990s when anywhere between 600,000 and 3 million North Koreans died, the social contract of North Korea changed.

Before, the government would tell the people be loyal to us, worship the leader, you will be looked after. You will be fed and clothed through the public distribution system. Since the government is no longer able to do that and the public distribution system has collapsed outside of Pyongyang, the new social contract in North Korea is that if people are loyal to the regime and worship the leader they are allowed to seek limited economic opportunity. This is what happens at some of these sites overseas. The three supervisors at each site are also interested in making some money on the side. They are certainly corrupt so the party secretary, the State Security Department agent, the work site manager clear those workers who appear to be most trustworthy and allow them, for example, to approach a South Asian worker who gets paid $40 a day. The North Korean will take only $20 and basically the other worker will have $20 left to keep to himself and he might go ahead and do another job. In the meantime, other North Korean workers on the side have to make up for the level of effort of the North Korean who has been subcontracted by the foreign worker by working more. He comes back. He brings his $20. But, of course, he has to pay respects to the three site supervisors. He has to bribe them and he is left with very little at the end of the day. We have also come across reports of North Korean workers allowed to moonlight for other companies and, of course, they have to bring back money that is sent both to the authorities and they also have to bring back bribes -- money -- that is given to the site supervisor. So the difference is that some of them may have a little bit of money left, dismal amounts -- dismal amounts which might make a difference for the families left back home in Korea where $100 U.S. or $200 can get them a long way.

MR. PITTS. Thank you. Mr. Lim Il, I read your testimony. You worked in Kuwait for how many years?

MR. IL. I worked in Kuwait about five months.

MR. PITTS. Five months. And your working hours were from 7:00 in the morning, 11 hours a day plus night time work from 9:00 to 12:00 midnight -- 14 hours. Is that correct?

MR. IL. Yes, it is correct.

MR. PITTS. And how much pay did you receive when you worked? How much was your salary?

MR.IL. At all. I haven't received at all.

MR. PITTS. You never received any money for payment?

MR. IL. No.

MR. PITTS. What were you told about where your salary or your payment was going?

MR. IL. So I -- once I actually asked to my supervisor, who was actually a foreign national but he said that we already paid your salary to your company in North Korea.

MR. PITTS. Okay. And you say in your testimony there are 20,000 workers from North Korea in Kuwait?

MR. IL. So when I was working in Kuwait there was about 1,800 people -- workers, North Korean workers -- working in Kuwait and the number actually went up to 4,000 to 6,000 right now.

MR. PITTS. And you mentioned you had to go through several hours of indoctrination -- propaganda. How many hours of indoctrination did you have to go through a week?

MR. IL. So every Wednesday we had to take a one-hour education class and on Saturday we had to have an evaluation session which is basically criticizing each other's ideology and within two -- in two weeks every -- in two weeks of Friday we have to take the two-hour class for other ideology class.

MR. PITTS. And how many days a week did you have to work? Was it seven days a week or --

MR. IL. So we can only get a day -- a half day off within the two weeks -- once in two weeks.

MR. PITTS. One half day every two weeks?

MR. IL. Exactly.

MR. PITTS. Now, how would you describe your situation? I asked the ambassador how he described overseas worker programs -- if they were human trafficking, if it would be classified as slave labor. How would you classify your overseas work program?

MR. IL. I think we are the slave laborers of the North Korean regime.

MR. PITTS. Slave labor. Which countries and in which industries are overseas North Korean workers experiencing the worst conditions, in your opinion?

MR. IL. I consider the workers in the Middle East countries including Kuwait and Qatar, which 10,000 North Korean workers are working right now, might be the worst case, among the worst environment among all North Korean overseas workers.

MR. PITTS. Now, can you provide any examples of U.S. companies or U.S. entities who are benefiting from labor by overseas North Korean workers?

MR. IL. Not at all.

MR. PITTS. None. All right. Thank you very much. Your testimony is very compelling.

MR. SIFTON, I will go to you. How can international organizations such as the United Nations or the International Labor Organizations contribute to curtailing human rights abuses against North Korean overseas workers?

MR. SIFTON. Well, starting with the International Labor Organization, which my colleague mentioned earlier, this is a group which does different things in different countries, has pilot programs which are funded by governments or by different donors, some of which could be brought to bear on these situations that we are discussing here today. It is, you know, some of the smaller cases that we have but there are workplace inspection programs in Cambodia that the International Labor Organization does for garment factories in Cambodia. Why it can't include one or two North Korean restaurants into the mix, it is not that much work. Granted, it is not that many workers but the revenue streams are enormous. These South Korean tourists spend enormous amounts of money. They give enormous tips to these restaurants and per worker the revenue streams are quite big and, you know, this might be a way to put a crimp in that revenue stream. So that is one way. The other thing is just to simply encourage labor rights organizations working in the various countries to focus a little bit more on this. South Asia gets a lot of attention because in places like Kuwait and Qatar most of the workers are from South Asia countries, not from places like North Korea, and they put most of their attention on those countries, with good reason. But there is no reason why those local labor rights groups can't be encouraged to focus more on North Korean workers as well.

MR. PITTS. The operations of North Korean industries and the working conditions for laborers inside the PRNK are opaque. However, we do get a clear picture of Pyongyang's policies by observing the operation of the Kaesong Industrial Complex. Can you tell us what your organization has observed with respect to this complex?

MR. SIFTON. Well, Kaesong is a very difficult case because on the one hand, recently, North Korea has requested that the so-called wages for the workers there be increased and from a labor rights perspective you initially at a sort of first blush glance think okay, well, that's a good thing. But given what we know and what has been alleged about the extent to which those wages are taken by the North Korean government it looks like nothing more than just an effort to make more money out of the -- off the complex, and whether that would actually accrue to the workers themselves is very difficult to say and I, for one, am pessimistic that it would.

What we have suggested to the South Korean government and to South Korean corporations is that they use their power to negotiate for better transparency on that issue. It is very difficult, of course, to monitor. Transparency is a very difficult thing to obtain in a situation like Kaesong. But they could ask for more in terms of the monitoring of the workers and the efforts to get the money directly to them and their families. I'm not a lot

-- you know, again, not optimistic about that but at least they could try and that is what we have encouraged South Korea and South Korean corporations to do. Unfortunately, however, we are seeing that some of the South Korean corporations are already folding under pressure and are agreeing to pay the higher wages which, again, they are not really wages but merely fees that the North Korean government takes.

MR. PITTS. Now, you heard my question to Mr. Lim Il about U.S. companies or entities benefiting. I would like to ask you, Mr. Sifton, and you, Mr. Scarlatoiu, can you provide any examples of U.S. companies or entities benefiting from labor by overseas North Korean workers?

MR. SIFTON. We -- our research has not touched on that subject yet but I believe that information is obtainable and could be to obtained. That is why we are pressing especially for the trade agreements to include better avenues for that transparency. But I think that is a very important issue that needs to be addressed.
I also note you asked about the status -- trafficked labor versus slave labor.

MR PITTS. Yes. How would you classify?

MR. SIFTON. This is something we have, you know, wrestled with. But the bottom line is that the definition of slavery, in the Slavery Convention, for instance, is that the status of a condition of a person over whom ownership rights are exercised.

Well, ownership can be defined in different ways by the fact that a person is bought and sold or transferred for fees or by the fact that a person can be disposed of as the owner sees fit, which really means that anything can be done with the person without any accountability.

It may be that we have to use analogy to get there but given the almost divine control that the North Korean government exercises over its own citizens I think that the right of ownership can very easily be met in the sense that while it doesn't meet the ordinary capitalist definition of ownership it isn't as though there are slave markets in Pyongyang like there were two centuries ago. It is analogous to ownership in the sense that the North Korean government can dispose of its citizens however it sees fit.

MR. PITTS. Mr. Scarlatoiu, could you elaborate on those two issues as well? Do you know of any U.S. companies or entities benefiting from labor overseas and how would you characterize this labor?

MR. SCARLATOIU. Mr. Chairman, I have not come across such evidence at this stage. I have been primarily focused on the working conditions and the status of the human rights of these workers at these locations overseas. That said, we are dealing with global supply chains that depend on global consumption. There may be companies out there that they have no idea that some of these products have North Korean content.

We are also aware of another very serious issue, the use of forced labor in North

Korea's extractive industries. Our organization has documented the use of forced labor from the political prison camps, for example. There may be companies that are unaware that the content is there. So as far as action is concerned, I think that the first very important step would be to conduct a thorough research and investigation and get a very clear idea of where these supply chains are. It is certainly a very challenging issue, as was mentioned earlier.

MR. PITTS. Thank you, and how would you categorize the overseas worker programs, in your opinion? Is that a human trafficking -- state-sponsored human trafficking? Slave labor?

MR. SCARLATOIU. In most cases it could be qualified as forced labor. Certainly, what makes the analysis difficult is that these workers are not generally forced to take up these jobs. They volunteer, and as mentioned earlier, as terrible and appalling as working conditions may be, they still have the opportunity to make that little amount of money or at least they hope that they will have an opportunity to make their families' lives a little bit better. In many cases, they fail to do so. Some of them -- restaurant workers, for example, have told me that what they really wanted to do was to explore the outside world. They didn't really get a chance to do that because they were confined to their working and living quarters.

Now, certainly, what makes the case of North Korea unique, and this applies to illicit activities run by North Korea, for example, why are those North Korean super notes, the $100 bills, so well made? Why is the quality so good? Because other criminal organizations all over the world do this but in North Korea it is state assets that are used to produce this counterfeit currency. They use the same rolling presses used to produce North Korean currency.

In this particular case there are groups all over the world, criminal groups that run human trafficking rings. They are involved in forced labor. They are involved in sexual exploitation. In this particular case, it is state assets that are used to basically turning these North Korean workers into forced laborers and perhaps that is why the system is so dreadfully efficient. On the other hand, because we know that these are state assets and this is a state-run operation, compared to other operations run by criminal organizations this may present us with an opportunity to be able to target the locations and the particular modus operandi of these operations going on at locations in those 16 countries.

MR. PITTS. In your opinion, if you were members of Congress what should the U.S. Congress do or what would you recommend the U.S. government do to address this problem of overseas workers programs from North Korea? I will just go down the line. I will start with you, Mr. Scarlatoiu.

MR. SCARLATOIU. It is -- it is very important, Mr. Chairman, to remind those 14 out of 16 countries that they are members of the International Labor Organization. Yes, these work sites are managed by North Korean supervisors. Sometimes they are even allowed to exercise law enforcement functions inside the perimeter.

Nevertheless, this happens within the territorial jurisdiction of those respective countries and thus they are bound by their international obligations under the international covenant on civil and political rights, under the U.N. Universal Declaration of Human Rights and under their obligations as ILO member states to seek ways to improve the status of these workers, to seek ways to improve the status of all foreign workers all inside their national jurisdiction and especially the situation of North Korean workers.

It is important, I think, to take a close and careful look at this issue of forced labor affecting North Korean laborers overseas when we consider legislation that might address in the near or remote future, for example, sanctions against North Korea. And I think that it is also important to remember that this might be an opportunity.

Mr. Chairman, I have been a student of the Korean Peninsula for the past 25 years. I am a skeptic amongst skeptics. Nevertheless, with tens of thousands of North Korean workers overseas, the reason why they are there in the first place is that they do not know anything about human rights. They have no idea that they have human rights or labor rights.

I would recommend seeking ways to persuade those hosting countries, persuade NGOs, persuade employers organizations, labor unions and others to seek ways to reach out to the workers and inform them on their own human rights and labor rights embedded not necessarily in North Korean labor legislation and the North Korean constitution because they surely have their rights as citizens of North Korea -- but of course what is on paper is never applied to real life -- but inform them on the rights they have while residing within the territorial jurisdiction of those states.

MR. PITTS. Thank you. Mr. Lim Il, what would you recommend to Congress?

MR. IL. First recommendation is U.S. government should ask and persuade the countries -- the hosting countries not to receive any North Korean overseas workers in their countries. But if they have to they should -- the wages should be paid directly to the workers, not to the North Korean officials or regime, according to the international labor law.

MR. PITTS. All right. Mr. Sifton?

MR. SIFTON. I would like to strengthen this call for encouraging the ILO and labor groups that work in the countries in question to try to monitor and counsel these workers. It's a long shot but it is worth it.

One way that the U.S. Congress could compel that to happen is to insert into the appropriations bill a sense of Congress or an instruction or anything in the report text that basically instructs USAID and the State Department to use their program funding for ILO programs and other labor rights programs to include North Korea in the many other things they do.

If we got programs in Bangladesh to help workers there learn about their rights in the wake of Rana Plaza and other disasters there, we can have programs that are already looking at inspecting and counseling workers in other countries like Qatar and Kuwait to just include the North Korean workers in their workload. It is not a question of making them the only focus or, you know, prioritizing them but just including them in existing programs and getting that to happen, and I think all it would take is some language -- all it would take to get the ball rolling is language included in the appropriations markup and I am talking about the appropriations bill for foreign operations, in particular.

MR. PITTS. Thank you for that suggestion.

That concludes my questioning. I know the other members will have questions. They will send them -- I will send to you in writing if you would please respond. I am sorry that they are in other meetings because of what happened with our schedule. But, again, I would like to thank all of the witnesses who presented testimony today. We have had some very informative and important information shared with us and some good recommendations. I believe this was a useful discussion and tool of the commission in bringing about greater awareness to this issue. Hopefully, we will be able to bring more accountability to the People's Republic of North Korea and the host governments entering into these bilateral contracts.

The use of these agreements presents our government with many areas of concern and we have discussed the egregious working conditions of these laborers. We have also explored how these programs bring revenue to the regime in Pyongyang and one that uses these finances to further its repression of the North Korean people.

However, I do believe that this practice represents another problem for our government's foreign policy and our nation's effort to combat gross violations of human rights and that of an expanding geopolitical footprint of the PRNK. North Korea has been increasingly isolated in world forums as well as isolated from the global economy via U.S. and international sanctions and this growing practice of forced labor abroad disrupts these international efforts and the U.S. government and the international community, the intergovernmental organizations should treat this practice as an extension of the gross violations being committed by the regime in Pyongyang.

Furthermore, it must be understood that the revenues generated from these projects directly fund a regime accused of crimes against humanity. Governments and enterprises and individuals complicit in this practice not only support a violation of workers' rights but indirectly provide aid to the regime's repressive practices in the Korean Peninsula. So today we are calling for a general reform from policy makers in helping address this problem and to restate the attention that this commission will continue to devote to the plight of the people of North Korea and we will continue this investigation.

And with thanks to our witnesses, to all of those of you who have attended we thank you very much for your testimony and we will stay engaged.

And with that, this hearing is adjourned.

[Whereupon, at 5:11 p.m., the committee was adjourned.]

Appendix

North Korea's Forced Labor Enterprise:
A State-Sponsored Marketplace in Human Trafficking

Please join the Tom Lantos Human Rights Commission for a hearing on the Democratic People's Republic of Korea (DPRK)'s provision of forced labor to foreign governments through bilateral contracts.

Credible reports indicate that the DPRK's "contract workers" are sent to countries in East Asia, Central Asia, Africa and Central Europe and are forced to work while their movements are surveilled by DPRK "minders." Workers' salaries are deposited into accounts controlled by the North Korean government, which keeps most of the money, claiming various "voluntary" contributions to government endeavors. Workers receive only a fraction of the money paid to the North Korean government for their work.

In recent years, international condemnation of North Korea's government has been growing, including accusations within the United Nations of potential crimes against humanity by the regime in Pyongyang. However, the use of forced labor by the DPRK in fulfilling its international contracts may offer a new entry point for combatting the government's ever-growing list of human rights violations.

This hearing will bring together experts to discuss the causes and consequences of North Korea's use of forced labor abroad and provide recommendations on what the United States can do to protect these victims of state-sponsored human trafficking.

Panel I:

- **Mr. Robert King**, Special Envoy for North Korea Human Rights Issues, U.S. Department of State

Panel II:

- **Mr. Greg Scarlatou,** Executive Director, Committee for Human Rights in North Korea
- **Mr. Lim Il, Co-director,** International Network for the Human Rights of North Korean Overseas Labor
- **Mr. John Sifton,** Asia Advocacy Director, Human Rights Watch

This hearing will be streaming live at http://www.ustream.tv/channel/hclive22.

For any questions, please contact Carson Middleton (for Mr. Pitts) at 202-225-2411 or carson.middleton@mail.house.gov or Soo Choi (for Mr. McGovern) at 202-225-3599 or soohyun.choi@mail.house.gov.